Theological Malpractice?

*Essays in the Struggle
for United Methodist
Renewal*

by James V. Heidinger II

THEOLOGICAL MALPRACTICE?
Essays in the Struggle for United Methodist Renewal
© 2000 by James V. Heidinger II
Published by Bristol Books, an imprint of Bristol House, Ltd.

First Edition, March 2000

Unless otherwise indicated, all Scripture quotations are from the *Holy Bible, New International Version* © 1973, 1978, 1984 by the International Bible Society. Used by permission of Zondervan Publishing House.

ISBN: 1-885224-29-X

Printed in the United States of America

Bristol House, Ltd.
P.O. Box 4020
Anderson, Indiana 46013-0020
Phone: 765-644-0856
Fax: 765-622-1045

To order call: 1-800-451-READ (7323)

To my sons

Jay, Mark and Ryan

Contents

Foreword

· ·

EPISCOPALIANS, Presbyterians, Lutherans, and other major American denominations have stunningly similar problems and moral dilemmas. Anyone who reads this account of the struggle for doctrinal integrity within one Protestant denomination will easily see analogies within others.

The United Methodist Church has undergone tumultuous conflicts in the last three decades. While these conflicts are by and large replicated in every major Protestant denomination, they are especially acute among United Methodists, where these dilemmas are greatly magnified by the size of the denomination. Of all the mainline denominations related to the World Council of Churches, it is the largest.

Yet there has been a precipitous decline of United Methodist membership from 12.5 million in 1968 to 8.5 million today, during a time in which evangelical churches have grown exponentially. This decline shows evidences not merely of maladministration or stupidity or introversion, but more so of doctrinal apostasy and confusion and loss of seriousness about the Great Commission.

Many clergy and lay persons within American Protestantism have been praying earnestly for the renewal of theological integrity within their church bodies. This book presents evidences of these prayers, hopes, and struggles. It provides reasoned argument for a more biblical understanding of these grassroot issues.

During these years, no one to my knowledge has been a more astute observer of the confessing and renewing movements within liberal Protestantism than has James Heidinger. No one has kept a better archive of the facts of these controversies. No one has given them a more astute, cohesive, and thoughtful evangelical interpretation than he.

What this book brings together is the essence of his editorial forays and thoughts that explain the problems and possibilities of evangelicals, orthodox and traditionalists within a secularizing and demoralizing cultural environment to which their denominations have snugly and uncritically adapted. Thus it has ongoing pertinence to all those faithful lay Christians who are struggling with the same problems: the loss of doctrinal integrity, the collapse of theological education, the permissive sexuality issues, the overweening influence of radical feminism, the issues of fair representation, church finance and governance and bureaucratic accountability.

For the last 19 years James Heidinger has edited the frontline journal, *Good News,* that has best covered the scene of United Methodist doctrine and polity through these tumultuous days. It is the only journal that has had a sustained critical take on the UMC over the last few decades. Virtually all other sources for reporting Methodist activities and issues have been bought and paid for and are wholly owned subsidiaries of the UM bureaucracy against which evangelicals struggle for voice and integrity. Thus Heidinger's thoughts are of exceptional importance and value to all confessing and renewing Christians within mainline Protestantism.

For this reason I am grateful to be able to convey and commend them to you. I call liberals to a fair and honest reading of these arguments. I call evangelicals and orthodox to a renewed commitment to the one Lord of glory they seek to serve.

Thomas C. Oden

Preface

IF there is a theme that runs through the essays in this book, it is that the United Methodist Church, and mainline Protestantism in general I would add, have been tragically negligent of their rich doctrinal heritage. One of the remarkable features of the decade of the 1990s was the sheer number of theologians who traveled in great demand to tell mainline Christian audiences all the things they no longer believed about historic Christianity.

It is arguable that United Methodism has two different religions functioning under one large ecclesiastical tent. One faith would be traditional, historic Christianity and the other a mix of liberal teaching and New Age spirituality. That's why we have such difficulty agreeing on much of anything. A few years back, we decided we would name it "pluralism" or "diversity" and say it was a sign of our strength. We are told that these differences (and they are real differences!) are not really significant. We all should still be able to live under one roof. Let's just live and let live.

It struck me recently just how long this condition has existed within United Methodism. I was ordained an elder in 1969. I can remember hearing the same thing as I entered the ministry. During the past thirty years the revisionist themes have continued, changing very little. They go something like this: The Scriptures are of human origin, not divine; Jesus was not born of a virgin nor was he raised from the dead; Jesus never claimed divinity for himself and was no different from you or me; and humankind is basically good, not sinful; etc.

We've heard those themes from United Methodist theologians, read them in our publications, and spoken with distraught church members whose pastors have preached them from their pulpits. The only thing different today is the boldness with which these themes are espoused. They have always existed but for years they remained more subterranean—always there but not fully manifest. Today we hear the revisionist messages much more plainly and boldly, thanks to popular voices like John Spong, Marcus Borg, and the much publicized Jesus Seminar crowd.

As we hear unfounded speculation and questionable scholarship espoused in place of the great doctrinal heritage of the church, we wonder to ourselves "What has happened to the mainline church?"

Several months ago I was in the hospital for a second angioplasty, an amazing and delicate procedure. I recall being awake in the sanitized operating room while several doctors ran a fine wire into my left anterior descending artery to "balloon" it open and then placed another small stainless-steel stent in the artery to help keep it open.

As I reflected about that procedure, I realized that the one thing I wanted for sure was precision. That was no time for a sloppy, "hit and miss" procedure. I also wanted honesty. I wanted a doctor who could say to me confidently, "Jim, I know what needs to be done. I'm properly trained and can do the procedure well." What I didn't want was a doctor who would say lightly, "Well, they taught me about angioplasty in medical school, but I have my own theories. I don't like to be confined. I enjoy experimentation." Just the thought is laughable. Not on my arteries you won't!

At times I think that is how some in the United Methodist Church are approaching the task of Christian ministry, or "the cure of souls," as it used to be called. Many, like Wesley, still want to know "the way to heaven." But some clergy today would respond by beginning a debate about the existence of heaven. Others would speculate about the many and various roads that one can take to get there, all having equal merit. They, too, enjoy "experimentation" and don't want to be "confined" by the stuffiness of the biblical message.

Physicians would never be so careless in their medical practice. It simply wouldn't be allowed. They would be slapped with a malpractice suit in a moment, and rightly so. As I think about what the church has been doing with the message of the Gospel, I am convinced we are seeing "theological malpractice" in our handling of the Word of truth. People are coming to our churches Sunday after Sunday expecting in good faith to hear a sure and trustworthy message about the Christian life. Too often what they hear is a "mess of pottage" about mystery, relevance and left-leaning political ideology. Worshipers come seeking bread and get stones.

As persons today expect professionalism and competence from their doctors and physicians, parishioners deserve honesty, professional competence, and utter faithfulness to the Gospel from those who are its practitioners. Pastors should not only proclaim the biblical faith boldly and without apology, they should also live it consistently and with integrity. They should be a witness of its transforming power.

It's time to put an end to "Theological Malpractice." The stakes are too high. The covenant we have made is much too serious to be trifled with recklessly. The eternal destiny of those with whom we live and minister is far too great a trust to treat frivolously.

For the church to experience lasting renewal, it must recover fidelity to the content and substance of the Gospel. That is the unifying thread that runs through these essays. The various Declarations which I have included in the Appendixes are very significant statements signed by thousands of United Methodists calling for renewed faithfulness to the Gospel. I have references to most of them in this book. They are important documents historically as well, because they represent major grassroots efforts during the past 12 years to call United Methodist leaders to a new faithfulness to our Wesleyan theological tradition. We must not forget those efforts and the many United Methodists they represented.

Evangelicals know that renewal comes in answer to the prayers of God's people. Today, all across the church, thousands of United Methodists—and other mainline believers as well—are interceding specifically on behalf of their church for revival, renewal and reform. Statistician and missiologist, David Barrett, claims there are approximately 170 million believers praying for the revival of the church and for world evangelization. God hears those prayers and will respond in His good time, according to His purposes. So, let us join the mighty and growing grassroots prayer effort, pleading earnestly with the psalmist, "Will you not revive us again, that your people may rejoice in you?" (Psalm 85:6)

Along with our praying, let us address courageously the doctrinal defection that threatens to alter the very substance of the Gospel in our teaching and preaching. Let us make sure that our praying does not become a means of escape for us from the unpleasant task of obedience in identifying and confronting doctrinal unfaithfulness and reductionism when we see it in the church. Those of us who are clergy promised that in addition to preaching the Word of God faithfully, we would also "defend the church against all doctrine contrary to God's word." Admittedly, that task is not as pleasant and must be done with grace and wisdom, but it must be done.

My prayer is that these essays will help us all, United Methodists and our brothers and sisters who face similar struggles in the other mainline denominations, address more clearly the doctrinal and theological malaise that is at the heart of our denominational decline.

James V. Heidinger II
Nicholasville, Kentucky
October 1999

Acknowledgments

I want to thank my colleagues at Good News who have helped me consistently across the years be a better writer than I am. Their counsel, ideas, suggestions, and careful editing have been a great help to me in my regular writing responsibilities during my 18 years at Good News. I am deeply indebted to them all.

One

Theological Integrity and Doctrinal Recovery

Tradition, Reason, Experience Yield to Scripture

· ·

"One cannot say Scripture is primary and at the same time say Scripture, tradition, reason and experience are equal in importance and authority."

UNITED Methodism has an excellent new theological statement. The prominent theme ringing through it with bell-like clarity is the primacy of Scripture. This theme has replaced the controversial and problematic phrase, "theological pluralism," which the Hunt Commission purposefully omitted.

United Methodists will welcome the new statement and be encouraged by it. We all need to study the new document carefully. We need to discover just how pointedly the theme of "primacy" has been enunciated by the Hunt task force. Moreover, we need to be prepared to resist those who would cling to "theological pluralism," claiming little has changed for the church theologically. And that is already happening,

For example James Wall, United Methodist theologian and longtime editor of the *Christian Century,* has expressed concern about my comment that the church's new theological statement has eliminated the "doctrinal uncertainty" of the 1972 statement (see Wall's editorial in the May 18, 1988, issue). But he says he was reassured when he asked United Methodist seminary professor John Cobb whether the new statement rejected pluralism. Cobb said not really as long as reason, tradition and experience may be considered as both *criteria* and *sources* for doctrine.

Such a claim, however, seems more wishful than factual. For no less than nine times the new theological statement attests that in our theological formulation, Scripture is primary. That is, Scripture has the character of being first in time, order, rank; supreme; highest in authority; dominant, ultimate, final.

CLEARING UP THE QUADRILATERAL

The new statement clarifies that when speaking of Scripture, tradition, reason and experience—what we have recently called the Wesleyan quadrilateral—Scripture is unquestionably primary. To borrow Robert Tuttle's phrase, "Quadrilateral does not mean equilateral." This theme is pounded home in our new theological document. Note how tradition, reason and experience are subordinate to Scripture,

On tradition. The new document says, "Thus, tradition provides both a source and a measure of authentic witness, *though its authority derives from its faithfulness to the biblical message"* (italics mine). Obviously we struggle with good and reliable tradition as well as bad and unreliable tradition. How do we test them? Scripture. "Scripture remains the norm by which all traditions are judged." Tradition is indeed a criteria and source, but it is a secondary authority.

On reason. The new statement says Christian witness must "become our witness, it must make sense in terms of our own reason and experience." But under the section on "reason" we are reminded, "In theological reflection, the resources of tradition, experience, and *reason* are integral to our study of Scripture without displacing its [Scripture's] primacy for faith and practice." Reason is important but is always secondary to Scripture.

On experience. Experience is the "personal appropriation of God's forgiving and empowering grace." But again we are reminded "We interpret experience in the light of Scriptural norms . . . . In this respect, Scripture remains central in our efforts to be faithful in making our Christian witness."

The theme of Scripture's primacy is conspicuous by its repetition in the statement. Scripture is said to be "the constitutive [foundational, supreme] witness to the wellsprings of our faith," and it "occupies a place of primary authority among these theological sources."

Tradition, reason and experience may be cited as sources and criteria for theological formulation, but they are unquestionably subordinate to Scripture's supreme and authoritative place. Professor John Hick at the Clairmont School of Theology may believe it is *reasonable* to claim, as he does in his recent book, that there is salvation in all the great religious traditions of the world—Hinduism, Buddhism, Islam, etc. However, the authoritative message of Scripture overrules him. In such a case, reason must yield to Scripture's primacy.

A NEEDED CORRECTIVE

The Hunt Commission did not accidentally emphasize Scripture's primacy. It did so consciously to correct the sloppiness of our recent handling of the Bible. For far too long United Methodists have cited Scripture almost casually or incidentally—more as supplemental material than foundational. These days hungry church members could go a quadrennium without hearing a serious expository sermon from Romans, Ephesians or Colossians.

Some Christians say they accept Jesus as the supreme revelation of God, but they do not accept the authority of Scripture. But this leaves one with serious problems. How do we know Jesus was God's supreme revelation? How do we know what God was saying through Him? The truth is we would not know were it not for the Gospel narratives and the interpretations provided for us by the other biblical writers.

Therefore the Hunt task force has served our church well in articulating the primacy of Scripture with a sparkling clarity. Evangelicals will be vigilant to make sure it is not neutered by neglect or misinterpretation.

Let's keep the issue in focus. One cannot say Scripture is primary and at the same time say Scripture, tradition, reason and experience are equal in importance and authority. You just can't have it both ways. And about that the General Conference left no doubt.

Note: *At the 1988 General Conference, delegates adopted a new theological statement for the United Methodist Church, "Our Theological Task," which was brought to General Conference as the result of the work of a Theological Commission chaired by Bishop Earl G. Hunt, Jr. The new statement purposefully replaced the ambiguous and problematic guideline of "theological pluralism" with the clarifying theme of "the primacy of Scripture."*

July/August 1988

We Languish for Lack of Strong Leaders

· ·

"We languish today for courageous leadership. In fact some would say that leadership is actually courage in action. Courage denotes a heart and mind ready to act, ready for battle."

IT WAS a Monday morning in January 1982 that the Thunderbirds—the U.S. Air Force's spectacular stunt-flying team—suffered their most crushing disaster.

They were practicing the "Line Abreast Loop," in which four planes fly side by side, their wing tips as close as 18 inches, soar heavenward then gracefully arch backward until upside down and finally plunge toward earth in a perilous dive.

In all their maneuvers, only one of the four pilots—"the boss"—pays attention to where he is in relationship to the ground. The other three keep their eyes fixed on the boss's wing tip. When he goes up, they go up. When he goes down, they go down.

On this particular morning something went wrong with the boss's controls. He couldn't pull out of the dive. The other three pilots, their eyes fixed on their leader, waited for him to level off. They hit the floor of the Nevada desert in perfect formation at 490 miles an hour. All were killed instantly.

The story reminds us of the risks of leadership.

But any time people do anything together leadership becomes necessary. Nations need leaders. Businesses need leaders. And the Church of Jesus Christ needs pastors who are leaders. The Church has been strong when led and inspired by strong leaders.

William Willimon and Robert Wilson have written that the United Methodist Church needs leaders but what we have in the church today are managers *(Rekindling the Flame,* p. 59). The difference is obvious. Leaders are those others are following, but managers are those who "accept the validity of the institutional *status quo* and give their attention to its maintenance" *(Rekindling,* p. 59).

Leaders are able to inspire, direct, and influence the actions of others. They have the capacity to lead, guide and show the way others ought to go. Managers, however, often thwart bold initiatives by insisting that everything be done correctly, by the proper person and according to proper precedent.

The United Methodist Church is languishing today for lack of strong leadership. And as we hear of another staggering loss of members (72,000 in 1988), the image of those four jets crashing into the desert comes hauntingly to mind. At times I feel like shouting, "Is anyone watching the horizon? Does anyone see where we're headed? Are we locked hopelessly in formation in this downward dive?"

In his recent book *Signs and Wonders*, Bishop Richard B. Wilke says that since we have no pope or chief executive officer in the denomination, maybe renewal will have to come from "thousands of local church leaders who are recaptured by a vision of a world reborn in Christ Jesus" (p. 40).

And that could happen. But first these local church leaders, both pastors and lay, will have to lead the way in steering United Methodism away from some of its foolishness. Let me be specific:

Nearly everywhere you go United Methodist pastors and laity express their frustration at the growing trend of calling God "Father/Mother" or just "Mother." Seminarians report that it is safe to call God "Mother" but not "Father." Using the wrong language often brings one scorn from those who are "enlightened." Of course the controversial new God-language was never approved or adopted by General Conference, but it is being implemented nonetheless. And yet, while many privately express their deep dismay over the new God-language, few church leaders are willing to challenge it or even to raise the issue. Where is our leadership?

In addition, many United Methodist congregations are reeling in shock with pastors who have taken pro-gay stands, even advocating that homosexuals have the right to marry. This issue is splitting churches even as you read this. And this past July, at the Fellowship of United Methodists in Worship, Music and Other Arts, some 900 registrants heard the Gay Men's Chorus of Los Angeles perform and gave the singers "extended ovations." (The 70-voice chorus reportedly makes its home in the Hollywood and Wilshire United Methodist churches in Los Angeles.) While the 1988 General Conference delegates were clear in their votes on the matter of homosexuality, actions like those above continue to frustrate United Methodists and drive them out of the church. To be in ministry does not mean we give genial approval to behavior we have said is "incompatible with Christian teaching." Yet many are pushing to make homosexual practice acceptable in the church. Where is our leadership?

United Methodists are also distressed about some of the bizarre feminist theologies which have found their way into our denominational seminaries. They read of Rosemary Ruether at Garrett-Evangelical Seminary who consistently uses the term "God/ess" to express her belief that divine reality is best understood as an empowering "Primal Matrix," the great womb "in whom we live and move and have our being." Much of the new feminist teaching falls far outside the biblical tradition and will only confuse and divide local congregations. Some pastors and bishops privately express their shock and dismay at this questionable new fare being taught in our seminaries, but little else is done. Where is our leadership?

Some may say the above issues are not important; we must get on with the task of evangelism. To that I would say, "Yes, we must." But our church's pre-evangelism—that is, those messages and signals we send out prior to presenting the Gospel—hinders our entire evangelistic endeavor. In fact our image is so negative in some areas that local churches have been known to play down and even conceal their United Methodist connection on the signs in front of their churches.

We languish today for *courageous* leadership. In fact some would say that leadership is actually courage in action. Courage denotes a heart and mind ready to act, ready for battle. And Christians should understand that righteousness and truth must be fought for. Conflict is inevitable. We cannot be passive in the face of evil or wrongdoing. In fact, Israel's cowardice in the face of her opponents was seen as evil in the eyes of Yahweh. There was something ungodly about fearfulness; it was a sign of Israel's unfaithfulness.

What might happen were the church to heed Bishop Wilke's plea for "thousands of local church leaders" to be "recaptured by a vision of a world reborn in Christ Jesus"? It could help the United Methodist Church, headed like those jets in tight formation and in a perilous nose-dive, to pull out and begin to gain altitude once again.

For our denominational leaders to be bold and courageous, they must be sure of their faith and their relationship with God.

This requires a renewed commitment to lives of deep prayer and consistent study of the Scriptures.

For pastors it will mean casting off timidity for new boldness in preaching and teaching. Phillips Brooks, a giant of the pulpit in a previous generation, noted in his Yale Lectures on Preaching, "The timid minister is as bad as the timid surgeon. Courage is good everywhere, but it is necessary here. If you are afraid of men and a slave to their opinion, go and do something else. Go and make shoes to fit them. Go even and paint pictures which you know are bad but which suit their bad taste. But do not keep on all your life preaching sermons which shall not say what God sent you to declare but what they hire you to say."

Let's pray for and seek new, courageous United Methodist leaders whom God can use to move our church toward renewal and restoration.

September/October 1989

DuPage Declaration Calls for Biblical Fidelity

"Each issue mentioned [in the Declaration] contributes to the United Methodist Church's polarization. The DuPage Declaration is an attempt to get these issues before our various communions, and to show that strong consensus exists among evangelicals in the mainline churches."

IN MARCH a United Methodist conference on church unity was held. The headline from this gathering of leaders in interfaith efforts was that "liberal Christians seeking church unity must enter into dialogue with Christians in other cultures and with conservative Christians in the U.S." *(Newscope, 4/13/90).*

It is significant that dialogue with conservative Christians is mentioned in the same sentence as with Christians in other cultures. That may well reflect how far liberal Christians position themselves from evangelicals. Serious conversation with evangelicals is nearly a cross-cultural experience.

One United Methodist bishop at the church unity conference even claimed, "We have two parallel denominations within the United Methodist Church," referring to Good News. This was evidenced, he said, by the fact that Good News has its ". . . own seminary, publishing house, mission agency, and board of church and society."

Such a statement, though factually erroneous, does reflect the depth of division that exists within the United Methodist Church. Ours is not a "united" church. It cannot be until we all face the issues dividing our church.

At about the same time of that conference I was meeting with 21 evangelical renewal leaders to finalize and sign a document calling mainline Protestant churches to biblical fidelity. Named the DuPage Declaration, the document speaks to major theological and ethical standards under attack in mainline denominations. (See the Appendix III for the full text of the Declaration.)

I have met annually with these renewal group leaders for nearly a decade now. Though we come from diverse denominational backgrounds, our fellowship has an extraordinary unity. And we all speak of woefully little communication with the liberal leadership of our churches.

The critical issues we identify as polarizing our various denominations are quite similar. These include the loss of biblical authority, acceptance of new God-language, advocacy of abortion and homosexuality, a liberal leadership out of touch with a more conservative constituency, and more. It all sounds familiar, doesn't it?

The DuPage Declaration speaks to a number of the issues which are at the heart of our church's divided soul. In nearly every United Methodist debate we bear two very different, perhaps incompatible, views about Scripture's role in the life of the church. Evangelicals dismiss simplistic proof-texting; but they do insist that Scripture is the authoritative, written Word of God, not merely a human document which records the religious experiences of an ancient people.

The chasm on this issue is massive. United Methodist pastor Paul T. Stallsworth has noted that mainline liberal Christians have displaced classic Christian authority with that of "the autonomous individual." He rightly says that "under the sway of religious individualism, Scripture, as consensually understood through the creeds and confessions of the Church, [for the liberal] can no longer be taken to be authoritative. Instead *the individual's interpretation of Scripture,* usually without the assistance of confessions and creeds, becomes authoritative."

So for liberal Christians this "new authority" turns all debate about Christian truth and ethics over to the judgment of individual believers. Thus, subjectivism characterizes the debate and makes consensus impossible on most critical issues before the church.

United Methodism must not become a do-it-yourself religion. Privatizing the faith will bring utter confusion.

The DuPage Declaration also affirms the Trinitarian name of God—Father, Son and Holy Spirit. The renewal group leaders reported their denominations were being led, sometimes kicking and screaming, into the use of new language for the Godhead. Whether authorized or not, it is being implemented. Most saw their seminaries as unbending pockets of advocacy for the new language. They also reported that ministerial interview committees are quizzing new pastors about their willingness to use the new God-language. It's the new litmus test.

But liberal leaders need to know this is a bottom-line issue for evangelical Christians. "Creator, Redeemer, Sustainer" is an inadequate, thus unacceptable, alternative for the Trinitarian formula. Even so, United Methodist seminarians and pastors are being forced into using language that violates their consciences. Personally, I am increasingly offended by worship liturgy getting juggled to adapt to someone's ideological agenda or sensitivities. Why is there not equal concern about the sensitivities of everyone else?

We must ask again who has authorized these changes. The truth is, the United Methodist Church is presently in the midst of a concerted effort to change the way we address the Deity. Specifically, we are avoiding references to God as Father wherever we can. In our corporate liturgy we are seeking and using substitutes as often as possible. This pattern does not reflect careful theological understanding but rather a capitulation to feminist ideology.

The DuPage Declaration also affirms "the biblical guidelines for human sexuality" and denies "that premarital or extramarital relations, trial marriages . . . homosexual relations and so-called homosexual unions, can ever be in genuine accord with the will and purpose of God for his people."

For the renewal group leaders, these too are bottom-line issues. Compassion and ministry to homosexual persons. By all means. Acceptance of the behavior as an alternative lifestyle, no. Period. Yet all the mainline denominations have aggressive factions pushing acceptance.

One theme the renewal leaders came back to repeatedly was that the Christian Church needs to insist on correct data here. We are settling for undocumented opinions, letting them pass as facts. United Methodists must reject, outright, claims like (1) homosexuals can never change, (2) one in 10 persons is homosexual; (3) the Bible is not really clear about homosexuality; and (4) the behavioral sciences support the gay lifestyle.

In all the denominations the influence of the pro-gay faction far exceeds the numbers supporting it. Sentimentalism has replaced firm leadership.

The renewal group leaders also were unanimous in their opposition to abortion. Most would agree to a few exceptions in the "hard cases."

It is here the liberal leadership of the mainline churches, United Methodists included, have left a major moral issue in the hands of the "autonomous individual." They have said, in essence, "It finally boils down to the individual decision of the woman. We must protect her freedom of choice."

But surely this depends on just what it is that is being aborted. If we are talking about a bodily appendage, like tonsils or the appendix, there would be no issue, no controversy. Certainly it's the woman's choice. But if we are talking about a person, a child, that is a different matter. (Incidentally, in Latin *fetus* means offspring or unborn child.) Laws have always forbidden the taking of the lives of children. This decision cannot just be left to the choice or whim of the "autonomous individual."

Each issue mentioned above contributes to the United Methodist Church's polarization. The DuPage Declaration is an attempt to get these issues before our various communions, and to show that strong consensus exists among evangelicals in the mainline churches.

But make no mistake, we are a divided church. And a liberal United Methodist minority cannot continue to impose upon United Methodists doctrines, social views, and new God-language which we find questionable, disturbing, and personally offensive.

Note: *In October 1996, the renewal group executives mentioned above became the Association for Church Renewal (ACR). Having met for more than 17 years, they decided it was time for a more intentional organization. The ACR meets twice annually.*

May/June 1990

What To Do About "Other Gospels"

. . . .

"A pastor from one of our largest
United Methodist churches said in a
message recently that he could handle
the first phrase of the Apostles' Creed
but then he starts choking. He added
that if he takes the creed literally, he
has trouble with it. He uses it but says
he adjusts it with his own meaning."

How are the mainline churches doing? Well, they've had their problems, as we know. The five denominations usually considered "mainline" have lost five million members since 1965, while the U.S. population was growing by 57 million.

Author and theologian Richard John Neuhaus writes that among the strengths of the mainline/old-line denominations is an impressive number of vibrant congregations. That's true for United Methodism.

After noting other strengths, Neuhaus cites the mainline church's greatest weakness—its "uncritical cultural capitulation, of not making a clear distinction between the church and contemporary culture." But more sobering yet, he says we mainliners have fallen prey to apostasy by proclaiming "other gospels" *(Faith and Renewal* magazine, July/August, 1990, p. 4ff.).

That's a serious charge. What are these other gospels? Well, says Neuhaus, they usually take the form of one of several "transformative myths." They might teach a political transformation that will set aright the world's various ills. Or they might focus on a psychological transformation that helps "get our own act together" personally.

But are other gospels being preached within United Methodism? The evidence indicates so. Can we do anything about it? I believe so. Consider first some evidence.

A pastor from one of our largest United Methodist churches said in a message recently that he could handle the first phrase of the Apostles' Creed but then he starts choking. He added that if he takes the creed literally, he has trouble with it. He uses it but says he adjusts it with his own meaning. Before he finished he assured his listeners that Jesus didn't really turn water into wine at Cana.

Unfortunately, such mishandling of the biblical text is not new to us United Methodists. We hear these stories much too often.

Neuhaus also observes that "No single movement since World War II has had a greater impact on the churches than the sundry feminisms." And that strikes a familiar note. For one wonders what's lacking in the finished work of Christ that United Methodists feel the need to talk about the goddess Sophia, the earth goddess Gaia, or to invite a witch to lead a workshop on Dianic Witchcraft at a United Methodist seminary's women's week.

Why aren't more United Methodist leaders troubled by all this?

Maybe there's a reason few leaders have been upset. Neuhaus observes that the modern currents of theology view Scripture and tradition as basically a "troublesome treasure of symbolic resource, to be turned in whatever direction 'meets our needs'. . . Therefore, language about God, Christ, and the sacraments may be redesigned and tailored to conform to our sensibilities and felt urgencies." Is this how more and more of our leaders are viewing the Scriptures these days? Perhaps so.

Neuhaus concludes, "This is the most subtle form of apostasy. People continue to call themselves Christians and continue much of the language and ritual . . . but to an end that is fundamentally undermining of that which constitutes Christian faith."

Well, what can we do about it? I have a suggestion. One thing is to add your signature to the Louisville Declaration and urge others to do the same. (See the text of the Louisville Declaration in Appendix IV.)

What's the Louisville Declaration? It's a statement which calls the United Methodist Church to renewed faithfulness in both mission and evangelism.

The declaration affirms such basics as the uniqueness of Jesus Christ as the only Savior; it calls for renewed dedication to world evangelization and to lives of personal holiness. It contains major affirmations we seldom hear preached about these days.

Why a declaration? The answer is simple. It is yet another channel through which frustrated United Methodists can send a clear message to their leaders, whom they perceive as out-of-touch with their concerns. It's an attempt to say that we are a declining church, not because of poor programs or slothful stewardship, but because we aren't being faithful to the Gospel.

It's a chance to say that our United Methodist problem is not faulty communication or a flagging connectionalism. It's apostasy. We have imbibed other gospels. And the remedy is not some new quadrennial theme or programmatic emphasis, but rather confession, repentance, and seeking the power of God once again. You'll remember, the Apostle Paul had little tolerance for those preaching "another gospel" (see Galatians 1).

So the Louisville Declaration will be circulated throughout the church with the invitation for churches, classes, and individuals to sign their names to it. I urge you to do so and get others who will. Then send copies of letters with signatures to your bishop, district superintendent, and to the World Division head at our church's mission headquarters in New York.

What might result? Perhaps, under the Spirit's leading, we will see a new expectation emerge, one which insists that our pastors and theologians adhere to the historic Christian faith—I mean, really believe it and practice it. It is unfair, if not dishonest, to allow clergy to fill a pulpit Sunday after Sunday speaking about a faith they no longer embrace. And it's worse yet for clergy to claim they are being faithful when they know otherwise, redefining traditional doctrine with new, drastically different meanings.

To those leading us toward new theologies or conformity with the modern world, it's time United Methodist Christians said no in whatever ways it takes to make their voices heard. One good way is by a signature on the Louisville Declaration.

September/October 1990

A New Day for the Church?

"I would call that [emerging] new mood a growing impatience with theological fads, pet social and political agendas of our boards and agencies, and with our seeming capitulation to a relativistic sexual ethic."

ANNIVERSARIES are natural times to pause, reflect, evaluate, seek perspective and look ahead.

Twenty-five years ago this month, in March of 1967, Charles W. Keysor published the first issue of *Good News* and a renewal movement was launched. What a different world it was then. It seems so far away.

I finished seminary just two months after that first issue appeared and was ordained deacon and became a member of the East Ohio Conference. The American scene was volatile. Anti-war protesters appeared nightly on the news and the church was strangely willing to "let the world set the agenda."

The militant radical left was nearly the only show in town and the church was falling all over itself to accommodate it.

For many of today's tenured radicals in our universities, those days were "Camelot." To others of us, those days were chaos. The relativism of the "new morality" swept America like a prairie brush fire, and the church got scorched as it happened. Young people were warned not to trust anyone over 30. Long-standing moral values were abruptly swept aside, while main-line churches held the dustpan. We were told that "the newest was the truest and the latest was the best."

I am still amazed to recall that at one time there were *no groups or publications* which spoke on behalf of United Methodism's evangelical or conservative constituency. That helps explain the immediate flood of responses to Chuck Keysor's inaugural article, "Methodism's Silent Minority."

THE PROLIFERATION OF EVANGELICAL VOICES

It's a different world today and the United Methodist Church is not the same church. Think of the organizations that didn't exist 25 years ago. You have Good News, The Institute on Religion and Democracy, A Foundation for Theological Education, The Mission Society for United Methodists, The Transforming Congregations ministry, the Taskforce of United Methodists on Abortion and Sexuality (*Lifewatch*), the Evangelical Coalition for United Methodist Women (now RENEW), and even Don Wildmon's American Family Association. We should also include several groups affiliated with the General Board of Discipleship, including the Council on Evangelism, the Foundation for Evangelism, the National Association of United Methodist Evangelists, and United Methodist Renewal Services Fellowship (now Aldersgate Renewal Ministries).

These groups undoubtedly have diverse purposes. They do not all walk in lockstep, to be sure. *But let's not miss the significance of their existence.* The voices of United Methodist evangelicals and traditionalists are *finally* being heard.

Channels now exist to guarantee this will continue to happen. Thousands of United Methodists have found ways to address the spiritual, moral, theological and social issues that exist in their church.

AN EMERGING NEW MOOD IN THE CHURCH

These groups are a part of an emerging new mood in the United Methodist Church. I would describe that new mood as a *growing impatience* with theological fads, pet social and political agendas of our boards and agencies, and with our church's seeming capitulation to a relativistic sexual ethic.

Recently I read excerpts from a sermon preached by a church leader that expressed this kind of impatience. He said, "A powerful but influential minority is in the process of hijacking the doctrine, ethical teaching and worship of the church." And addressing those in the church whom he believed responsible for this, he continued, "If you wish to be allowed to perform single-sex marriages, reinterpret parts of the Creed, omit passages of Scripture which are unacceptable to you, or introduce feminist liturgies, then we shall not stand in your way, though we cannot worship with you."

The issues sound familiar, don't they? A United Methodist? No. The sermon was preached by the Venerable George Austin, the Archdeacon of York, one of the Church of England's most influential traditionalists. The story and excerpts from his sermon were published on the front page of London's *The Daily Telegraph* on September 9, 1991.

But Austin reflects the kind of growing impatience I discern among evangelicals within the United Methodist Church. Frankly, evangelicals are weary:

- Of the unending push to change the church's stand on the issue of human sexuality, including the support for gay and lesbian unions;
- Of United Methodist pastors publicly denying basic tenants of the Christian faith and not being disciplined for it;

- Of UM program boards continuing their participation in and support of the Religious Coalition for Abortion Rights (now the Religious Coalition for Reproductive Choice);
- Of prayers addressing God as "Bakerwoman," "Grandfather, great spirit," and "God our Father and Mother";
- Of position papers like one sent out recently from the Division of Ordained Ministry which has Jesus saying, "I am confused by your determination to make me the object of your worship and the guarantor of your salvation. You have never been lost and God is not angry at you."
- Of United Methodist clergy advocating worship of the goddess Sophia, authoring prayers, readings and a eucharist to this new-found deity.

I repeat, United Methodists are growing impatient with this kind of nonsense. I could be wrong but I believe this growing impatience is a major reason why 80 United Methodist leaders gathered in Tennessee in January to refine and then sign a statement called the "Memphis Declaration" (see Appendix V).

THE CRY FOR LEADERSHIP

When United Methodists feel compelled to form alternative groups within the church; to gather at their own expense to issue declarations to the church, as they did at Houston in 1987 and Memphis in 1992, what you have is a plea for leadership and a cry that enough is enough! One wonders at the silence of our United Methodist bishops amidst so much silliness. What has happened to the teaching and overseeing function of bishops, who according to Paul "must hold firmly to the trustworthy message as it has been taught," so they can "encourage others by sound doctrine and refute those who oppose it" (Titus 1:9).

One wonders whether any bizarre theological claim exceeds the bounds of acceptable limits today. Is anything so extreme as to be viewed as unacceptable?

I recall reading about C. S. Lewis' words spoken to a group of Anglican priests years ago. How timely they remain. He said, "It seems to the layman that in the Church of England we often hear from our priests doctrine which is not Anglican Christianity. . . It is not, of course, for me to define to you what Anglican Christianity is—I am your pupil, not your teacher. But I insist that wherever you draw the lines, bounding lines must exist, beyond which your doctrine will cease either to be Anglican or to be Christian: and I suggest also that the lines come a great deal sooner than many modern priests think. I think it is your duty to fix the lines clearly in your own minds: and if you wish to go beyond them you must change your profession. This is your duty not specially as Christians or as priests but as honest men" *(God In The Dock,* pp. 89–90).

We must ask, does United Methodism have any bounding lines today? If so, are they clear? And are they being enforced? It would appear not.

A NEW DAY FOR UNITED METHODISM?

I have written several times of the need for a new atmosphere within the church that expects from our clergy fidelity to Christian doctrine. It may be that such a new atmosphere is emerging. A hundred thousand signatures in the next two months affirming the "Memphis Declaration" would make an emphatic and unequivocal statement that such is happening. [*Note:* More than 212,000 signatures were garnered affirming the "Memphis Declaration." See Appendix V for the text of this document.]

And actions at General Conference in May could do the same. Were delegates to authorize moving the General Board of Global Ministries out of New York City, reject the Homosexuality Task Force Report, reduce the bureaucracy of the denomination, and terminate our involvement with the Religious Coalition for Abortion Rights, the church would feel seismographic shock waves from a membership that had finally learned how to speak.

Yes, United Methodism still faces serious problems. But it's a new day in many important ways.

Five years ago I concluded my editorial in the 20th Anniversary issue with words that are still relevant today: "Evangelicals today believe the church has been entrusted with a divinely revealed plan of redemption. This message is set forth clearly in the Word of God. This fact automatically establishes the relevance of the Christian message. We must resist attempts to impose other standards of relevance upon it. And even the slightest mishandling of that biblical message must be ruled out of order. If we are not faithful in the preaching of this historic faith, we will not 'Catch the Spirit' but will most assuredly 'quench the Spirit.'

"The Biblical message, proclaimed in the power of the Holy Spirit, *will* bear fruit. It will revitalize and renew United Methodism and enable us to share in the evangelical awakening that already is sweeping our land. And when our pulpits are alive again with the faithful proclamation of the Word of God, we can be sure the Lord will once again add daily to United Methodism those who are being saved."

March/April 1992

How United Methodists Do Theology

Missing ... is any hint that the issues raised by the Memphis Declaration have any validity. They apparently view the signers as persons insecurely clinging "to past forms."

IN 1972, eminent theologian Albert C. Outler urged United Methodists to "do theology." But the truth is, we don't do it very well. The responses seen thus far to the Memphis Declaration provide an important glimpse into just how the United Methodist Church deals with theological issues. I have wondered, frankly, whether United Methodist leaders are capable of serious theological dialogue in a context of mutual respect. Or, have denominational leaders lapsed into the unbecoming habit of responding to theological matters with the *ad hominem* response—that is, by attack or caricature of the critic rather than by addressing the issues? Unfortunately, we see too much of this in the various responses to the Memphis Declaration. (See Appendix V for the text of this declaration.)

One of the first printed responses to the Declaration was a "Here I Stand" piece in the *United Methodist Reporter* (April 10, 1992) by the Rev. Joe Sprague, a pastor in the West Ohio Conference and a delegate to General Conference. [Sprague was elected bishop in 1996.]

His piece is remarkable for what it makes of the Declaration and its signers.

From Sprague's article, we are told that to present Christ as God's unique gift of salvation to all humanity is to "limit God's grace" and was "to urge Christians to behave in a very un-Jesus-like manner." Our exclusivism "makes Jesus an idol, thus robbing God of the glory due God's holy name." We are told the Declaration "engages in bibliolatry, thus fashioning yet another idol which stands in place of the Holy One." The words of the Bible are "inspired but human, of eternal value yet time-bound and culturally conditioned."

Concerning God-language, the statement's views would make of it "yet another in a panoply of modern idols." The signers are seeking to "keep God securely contained in our own familiar language boxes." Concerning the Declaration's call to reject the Homosexuality Study Report, Sprague comments that "many of us can remember much of the same emotion, vehemence and biblical proof-texting when Blacks sought equality in the church . . ." He then asks, "Why such fear of differences?" (The signers obviously suffer from "differophobia.")

What one misses in Sprague's piece, circulated nationally, is any hint that the issues raised in the Memphis Declaration—signed by 100 United Methodist leaders, including five bishops, and by 200,000 United Methodists—have *any* validity whatsoever. From his response, Sprague believes the signers are engaging in idolatry and bibliolatry, are fearful of any God-language change, and are proof-texting on the homosexual issue. Frankly, Sprague treats the Declaration's concerns as frivolous—laughable, if not absurd.

A similar response to the Declaration came from 20 lay and clergy General Conference delegates from the California/Pacific Conference. According to their statement released in March, the signers of the Declaration have a spirit of "clinging to past forms and closure against free discussion." The California response speaks of older people who "try to sanctify the dominant social attitudes of the time when they were young." Concerning sexuality, we are told that "legalistically repeating teachings that were formulated by past generations, during a time when Christians did not affirm human sexuality as truly good, will close us to the new truth to which the Spirit calls us." It warns that "to cling to past forms that now oppress us more than they serve us is to reject God's offer of life."

Finally, we are instructed that "we live in a time when Christianity is no longer the one obvious bearer of enlightenment and salvation."

Missing again is any hint that the issues raised by the Memphis Declaration have any validity. They apparently view the signers as persons insecurely clinging to "past forms."

In one of the few episcopal comments we have seen about the Declaration, one NC [North Central] Jurisdiction bishop said in an interview that the world is changing and that these kinds of statements "grow out of desperation" as we seek "a place to stand in a world that is all too fluid." Again, one looks for some hint that the Memphis Declaration speaks to vital theological issues which need clarification in the church. What we hear are comments about persons who are basically insecure in a fast-changing world. That is insulting to those trying to present a thoughtful statement of concerns to the church.

No, we don't "do theology" very well. One wonders why many avoid discussing the rich, theological truths that undergird the church's ministry. Is it because some United Methodist leaders have, well, abandoned those foundational truths?

Believing the central doctrines and creeds of the church is a part, obviously not all, of what it means to be a Christian. They must never become options. In the words of British journalist William Oddie, "The great doctors of the Church have always restated the faith for their own time. But not one of them would have contemplated . . . the proposition that developments in human knowledge could conceivably alter the substance of what was being taught, or in any way modify the revelation once for all delivered."

A document signed by 200,000 United Methodists expressing concern that "there has been a falling away from commitment to the basic truths and doctrines of the Christian faith" deserves more thoughtful response.

July/August 1992

What Should Bishops Do?

· ·

*"If United Methodist bishops don't accept
the charge to hold the church accountable
to its doctrine, who will do it? Like it or not,
they are the custodians of the church's
Scriptural truth."*

THE United Methodist Church elected 16 new bishops in July. This is a good time to ask, "Just what do United Methodist bishops do?" Well, many things. They oversee the spiritual and temporal affairs of the United Methodist Church. They are to lead the church in its mission of witness and service in the world. They also are responsible for fixing pastoral appointments, which takes about 50 percent of their time, they say. Sometimes they address important social issues through pastoral letters to the church. At times we wonder if the bishops themselves understand their primary role in the church.

The bishops of the Episcopal Church acknowledged recently that they have no agreed-upon understanding of what it means to be a bishop. They met this past March to try to regroup after fierce feuding over human sexuality at their General Convention a year ago. They admitted they were in a state of disarray—nearly dysfunctional. Some admitted that real agreement may be impossible because Episcopal bishops do not share a common theological ground. South Carolina Bishop C. FitzSimons Allison said that many Episcopal bishops lack "an adequate understanding of Scripture as absolute authority. Most believe in a Hegelian view of progressive revelation that leads to Jesus Christ not being the only way." That is a candid admission and might well be said about some United Methodist bishops.

What, then, are our bishops supposed to do? We get a clue in the second question asked them in the service of consecration. According to our new *Book of Worship,* each is asked, "Will you guard the faith, order, liturgy, doctrine, and discipline of the Church against all that is contrary to God's word?" The next question asks if they will "proclaim and interpret to them [other ministers] the Gospel of Christ . . . ." Both questions are remarkably theological. Perhaps we shouldn't be surprised. Episcopal priest, Bruce McNab (Denver), says church history shows that the Anglican communion "has always had not only a reverence for the role of bishops, but in fact a dogmatic presumption that bishops. . . are the sacred custodians of orthodox doctrine, the guarantors of the Church's apostolic nature."

This helps us understand why Episcopal bishops have been frustrated with maverick bishop John Spong who recently ordained a known homosexual priest and has also questioned such basic tenets of Christian orthodoxy as the Virgin Birth, the divinity of Christ and the authority of Scripture. About the errant antics of Spong and several other Episcopal leaders, Bishop William Frey said, "Most of the bishops agreed they were sick of three or four members of the House [of Bishops] being the tail that wags the dog. The bishops wanted to find some way of holding each other accountable . . . We sensed a failure in courage in the leadership of the House of Bishops in doing that."

A major task of a bishop is to hold the church—its pastors, staff and lay leaders—accountable for the faith, order, doctrine and discipline of the church. That should include one another. Not only does the United Methodist service of consecration cite the function of doctrinal oversight, but so do the Scriptures. Paul says church leaders must "encourage others by sound doctrine and refute those who oppose it" (Titus 1:9). To refute, we should note, means "to prove to be wrong or false." A not-so-pluralistic task.

Unfortunately, this aspect of episcopal duties gets almost no mention in the interview process. What is discussed is leadership style, process, vision, goals and priorities. Little is said about seeing to it that the church remains faithful to its historic doctrine. But Cardinal Ratzinger reminded Catholic bishops recently that they are not on good biblical grounds serving simply as "moderators." Authoritative teaching, he insists, is the job of bishops—"even at the cost of popularity, even at the cost of martyrdom."

If United Methodist bishops don't accept the charge to hold the church accountable to its doctrine, who will do it? Like it or not, they are the custodians of the church's Scriptural truth.

Of course, doctrines and creeds don't encapsulate fully the great mysteries of the eternal God. But that does not make them any less essential. As British correspondent William Oddie has written, "A navigation chart of the Atlantic Ocean does not even begin to plumb the mysteries of those mighty waters. But the chart is, nevertheless, entirely true. A navigator who follows it will successfully cross the Atlantic; one who decides to enter into dialogue with the passengers to ascertain how they see the problem may succeed in steering his ship to the Statue of Liberty—but the chances are overwhelmingly against it."

Let's pray for our bishops that they will help lead United Methodism out of its doctrinal and theological malaise.

September/October 1992

Theological Malpractice?

. . . .

"Let's be done with the trendy 'theological bungee-jumping' which only entertains a watching crowd with some new, breathtaking theological novelty."

A THEOLOGIAN the magnitude of Tom Oden comes along only once in every two or three generations. Commenting on the United Methodist theological scene, Oden says, "We are cursed with the cancerous growth of a toxic doctrinal pluralism that lacks attentiveness to the unity of the classic tradition."

Is he overstating? We think not. One sees this "toxic" pluralism, for example, in theologian John Hick's calling for a "global religious vision," claiming it's no longer necessary "to insist . . . upon the uniqueness and superiority of Christianity, and it may be possible to recognize the separate validity of the other great world religions." Or, more simply, Christianity is no more viable or redemptive than, say, Hinduism or Islam.

The common thread running through most of the new pluralistic theologies, says theologian Donald Bloesch, is the denial that the man Jesus Christ is very God himself: a denial of our Lord's deity.

Hearing such views, one wants to protest, "What? Christ not divine? The great world religions as equally valid as Christianity?" What has happened to mainline theological education? Physicians would never be so careless in their medical practice. It wouldn't be allowed. Perhaps it's time to consider theological malpractice suits. We may smile, but remember the worshipers who come to our United Methodist churches Sunday after Sunday, many earnestly seeking (and deserving) a sure word from God.

Well, how are the seminaries doing? What sure word is being taught? Dr. Jon D. Levenson, professor of Jewish studies at Harvard Divinity School, gives us a disturbing glimpse (see *Christian Century*, February 5–12, 1992, pp. 139ff.). While at a conference recently, Levenson dined with several other Jews and a Christian professor from a prominent liberal seminary. The lone Christian professor told how his seminary had long ago given up its church affiliation, having embraced views beyond the denomination's "deepest beliefs."

"Are there, then, any beliefs or practices required of the faculty or students now?" asked one of the group. "No," replied the seminary professor firmly. But then, as an afterthought, he added, "except the requirement to use inclusive language."

Levenson, himself a Jew, seemed disturbed by this strange scenario. That, in an institution once explicitly Christian and still dedicated to the education of Christian ministers, one "can deny with utter impunity that Jesus was born of a virgin or raised from the dead. But if one says that he was the son of God the *father,* one runs afoul of the *institution's deepest commitments*" (emphasis ours).

Levenson went on to observe that the historic liberalism of that seminary had capitulated under the force of a new orthodoxy, that being a feminist orthodoxy of which "inclusive language" is the sign or symbol.

And it sounds so familiar. Our United Methodist seminaries may capitulate on the authority of Scripture or the deity of Christ. But when it comes to God-language, watch out—there's no wavering about this. Christ's deity, maybe. Inclusive language, absolutely!

The tragedy is that mainline theological seminaries have lost the unifying force of classic Christian doctrine. Thus, there is no common conceptual framework around which dialogue and debate can take place. Into this vacuum has come the new dogma of "political correctness" providing a new conceptual framework for seminaries, based on leftist ideology. And with it comes the arrogance of absolute certainty on the part of left-leaning intellectuals that sees opposing positions [to theirs] scarcely worth considering.

But the failure of the politically correct, according to professor Levenson, "lies in having drawn the circle of possible positions so tightly that education degenerates into indoctrination and the ritualized reaffirmation of self-evident truths—self-evident, that is, to those whose 'consciousness' has been 'raised.'" This has the disastrous effect of "excluding alternative positions from consideration, *or even expression,* as is increasingly the case on campus" (emphasis ours).

For many mainline seminaries, a *political absolutism* expressed through rigorous enforcement of "politically correct" speech and thought has rushed in to fill the vacuum left by *religious relativism.* Yes, the seminaries have their absolutes today. But they are drawn from politically correct ideology, not from classic Christian orthodoxy.

We are called to be faithful stewards of a great theological heritage. We must not fiddle with, embellish or try to improve upon that heritage. Let's be done with the trendy "theological bungee-jumping" which only entertains a watching crowd with some new, breathtaking theological novelty.

Rather, as Paul urges, we must "Guard the good deposit that has been entrusted to you" (2 Timothy 1:14). We must not sell a tested and true theological birthright for a mess of pottage called relevance.

January/February 1993

The World Council of Churches and Us

"The Bangkok Conference called for the Christian churches of the West to declare a 'moratorium' (an indefinite suspension) on its cross-cultural missionary activity. In other words, stop sending missionaries."

WELL, we're at it again. Another *Reader's Digest* (February 1993) article criticizing the World Council of Churches (WCC), followed by a lengthy United Methodist news release assuring us there's no reason to believe the *Digest's* irresponsible charges.

Newcomers need to know this controversy with the WCC is nothing new. More than a decade ago, Dr. Helmut Thielicke, a German Lutheran theologian of great stature and integrity, deplored the fact that "the World Council with its unilateral support of left-wing guerrillas and terrorist groups threatens to become increasingly a political club instead of a representative of the church."

The late Paul Ramsey, prominent United Methodist moral philosopher at Princeton University, rebuked the WCC for having "disregarded the most reliable available information and instead turned to the diagnosis and the recommendations of a secular ideology, including ideologies influenced by Marxism."

In recent years I have told those who are upset by the WCC that the council does not *cause* the problems of the mainline churches, rather it *reflects* those problems, which are first of all theological. Most evangelical critiques of WCC actions and statements seem applicable to the United Methodist Church. The WCC talks and sounds like our denominational leadership and reflects its theological confusion.

Well, how serious are the WCC's (and United Methodism's) problems, theologically? Several years ago, a major editorial in the respected evangelical journal *Christianity Today* examined the work of the WCC to see if it might merit evangelical support.

Editors Kenneth Kantzer and V. Gilbert Beers summarized the teachings within the WCC that have troubled biblically oriented evangelicals. Here's what they found: (1) Teachings on the deity of Christ are unclear; (2) The New Testament gospel had gotten lost—that is, that Jesus Christ, the divine Savior and Lord, became incarnate, died on the cross and rose again bodily from the dead to redeem mankind from sin through personal faith in himself; (3) The Bible had become an honored book used only for occasional proof texts but not for authoritative teaching; (4) Universalism—the view that all will be saved—had become standard doctrine for WCC teaching; (5) World history was interpreted in Marxist terms, glossed over with traditional Christian vocabulary; (6) Left-wing offenses against human rights and freedom were seldom noted or rebuked, but right-wing oppression was made a *cause celebre.*

The above concerns forced the editors to conclude that because the WCC failed to teach what is "essential to biblical Christianity," they must continue to oppose it.

In a more recent issue of *Christianity Today,* respected Anglican author and theologian, J. I. Packer, explained why he cannot support the WCC. Packer claims the Bangkok Conference on World Mission in 1973 marked a serious change of direction for the WCC. At Bangkok, salvation was equated with socio-politico-economic well-being. Reconciliation to God, sanctification by grace, and hope of eternal glory were no longer viewed as central—and for all practical purposes, were pushed aside. The Bangkok Conference called for the Christian churches of the West to declare a "moratorium" (an indefinite suspension) on its cross-cultural missionary activity. In other words, *stop sending missionaries.*

At Bangkok, the WCC officially embraced Universalism, the view that all will be saved. Thus, the tasks of mission and evangelism are merely options for the church, with little sense of urgency.

The WCC's euphoria about the Bangkok conference brought Packer to the painful conclusion that the council had become both irrelevant to and useless in the furthering of the church's God-given role.

Packer's critique fits United Methodism. Sadly, many of our denominational leaders affirm those same liberal missional views celebrated at Bangkok, including socio-political salvation, Universalism, and a moratorium on sending missionaries (the UM mission force overseas has dropped from 1,500 to under 500 in the past two decades). Somehow, the good news of the gospel has gotten lost. Our General Board of Global Ministries, the church's official mission-sending agency, is not simply *affected* by the WCC, it is a *partner* with it in theological defection.

Today, United Methodist leaders avoid substantive theological debate, perhaps for fear that others will discover what they no longer believe. But United Methodism will not experience renewal with insipid talk about ambiguity, mystery, and pluralism. Renewal will come only when the truth of the gospel "that Christ died for our sins according to the Scriptures, that he was buried, that he was raised on the third day according to the Scriptures" (1 Corinthians 15:3–4) is proclaimed again in power from our pulpits.

Equivocation on those foundational themes is what ails the WCC—and the United Methodist Church.

May/June 1993

Public Relations Won't Help the UM Crisis

· ·

"There is a perception by a growing number of United Methodists that our church is in a state of doctrinal free-fall with a leadership unwilling to face the crisis."

IN HER keynote address to the fall board meeting of United Methodist Communications, the Rev. Judy Weidman, new chief executive, spoke of a "tragic disconnect" between churchwide agencies and local congregations. Two priorities established by the communications group include (1) greater "visibility" for the denomination, and (2) raising money for churchwide programs and special funds.

To address those priorities, a Boston public-relations firm has been hired to place United Methodist spokespersons in the media, and shifts have been made toward a new approach to promote churchwide funds.

While there is something to be said for greater visibility and better public relations, the question must be asked whether this adequately gets at the heart of the problem. Will this really address the "tragic disconnect," the malaise we see within United Methodism?

Prior to the 1988 General Conference, a group of United Methodist evangelicals met and issued a statement of concern called "The Houston Declaration." In 1992 another statement was issued called "The Memphis Declaration," subsequently signed by a whopping 212,000 United Methodists! Last April [1994], evangelical United Methodist leaders met in Atlanta to discuss the denomination's theological crisis, resulting in the formation of a "Confessing Movement" within the United Methodist Church.

In the initial statement from Atlanta, "An Invitation to the Church," some 85 respected, loyal United Methodist leaders signed on to declare that "The United Methodist Church is at a crossroads." Further, the reason for the crisis is "our abandonment of the truth of the gospel of Jesus Christ as revealed in Scripture and asserted in the classic Christian tradition and historic ecumenical creeds. . . . Specifically we have equivocated regarding the person of Jesus Christ and his atoning work as the unique Savior of the world. We have been distracted by false gospels."

The situation is so critical that these 85 leaders, including two active and three retired United Methodist bishops, felt something must be done. Their plan: "In order to enact the *Discipline's* call to 'doctrinal reinvigoration' and to avoid schism and prevent mass exodus, we intend to form a Confessing Movement within the United Methodist Church. By this we mean people and congregations who exalt the Lordship of Jesus Christ alone, and adhere to the doctrinal standards of our church." These 85 leaders are not sideline critics but effective pastors and respected leaders with impeccable records of service and loyalty.

Who they are gives great credibility to what they have said. And what they have said is serious stuff. Another word for "abandonment of the truth of the gospel," I would remind you, is "apostasy." To avoid "schism" and prevent "mass exodus" are strong words implying a crisis so serious that it will not be helped by better public relations.

There is a perception by a growing number of United Methodists that our church is in a state of doctrinal free-fall with a leadership unwilling to face the crisis; some leaders are, themselves, a part of the problem. Even after seven years, two widely-circulated declarations, and the forming of a Confessing Movement, most United Methodist bishops are unwilling to acknowledge any theological crisis; and they seem to be dismissing the Confessing Movement as much ado about nothing.

What might be done? A positive first step the Council of Bishops might consider would be to invite a group of 15–20 evangelical leaders (not one or two) to meet with the Council at one of its upcoming meetings, giving *a whole day* to listen to their concerns. Let the evangelical leaders explain as best they can what necessitated a Houston Declaration, a Memphis Declaration, and a Confessing Movement. Let them make presentations to the Council, meet with bishops in small groups, eat together, and pray together about this church and its struggles.

Frankly, I am baffled by the fact that it hasn't already happened. With all of our concern about inclusivity, the denomination's continued resolute distancing from its evangelical constituency—all the while urging it to be faithful in its financial support—is a contradiction of the church's claim to want inclusiveness.

With the unofficial Mission Society for United Methodists celebrating a ten-year anniversary of ministry (having more than 120 persons serving Christ in some 24 countries) yet unrecognized, unacknowledged, and unaccepted by most of our bishops, we are reminded that there is, indeed, a "tragic disconnect" within United Methodism.

For our bishops to launch *this* kind of bold "initiative" would encourage, perhaps even win back, many "disconnected"

United Methodists. If the bishops would follow through, we wouldn't need the public relations firm; and we might even see our church funds increase.

Note: *The full texts of the Houston Declaration, the Memphis Declaration, and the Confessing Movement's Invitation to the Church can be found in the Appendixes of this book.*

November/December 1994

A New Voice for Theological Renewal

· ·

"The Confessing Movement had made it clear earlier that it is not asking for 'a new definition of faith, but for a new level of integrity in upholding our historic doctrinal standards in a thoughtful, serious, and principled way.'"

EPISCOPAL theologian David Mills has said that when churches lose their shared beliefs and unexamined assumptions, they have lost that which integrates them and gives them cohesion. Mills believes this explains the decline in the mainline Protestant churches in America.

It was concern about such doctrinal loss within the United Methodist Church that brought 102 United Methodists to Atlanta in 1994 and led to the formation of the Confessing Movement Within the United Methodist Church. In April of 1995, more than 900 United Methodists gathered in Atlanta and joined in issuing the new movement's "Confessional Statement" which said, "The United Methodist Church is now incapable of confessing with one voice the orthodox Trinitarian faith, particularly Jesus Christ as the Son of God, the Savior of the world, and the Lord of history and the Church." The fact that some prominent United Methodist theologians and pastors have protested the Confessing Movement's call to confess Christ as Son, Savior and Lord perfectly illustrates the very theological crisis being addressed.

This past September 27 and 28, the Confessing Movement held a second national conference, meeting in Cincinnati, Ohio. The 500 persons attending acted with boldness and enthusiasm to (1) reaffirm the urgent need for the Confessing Movement, and (2) to move ahead to employ a full-time executive director and establish a central office, staff, and board which will allow the movement to expand its outreach and effectiveness.

Good News commends this action and welcomes the Confessing Movement into its new level of ministry. As we have done with other emerging ministries, we will offer whatever support and encouragement we can to help this new effort, referred to by Dr. Billy Abraham, professor of theology at Perkins School of Theology, as "one element in a fascinating network of renewal which is sweeping through our church as a whole."

Abraham preached during morning worship in Cincinnati and lifted a theme that will be heard often from the Confessing Movement: "Doctrine is essential for the *unity, spiritual welfare, and stability* of the church." With that, United Methodists evangelicals will heartily agree.

The Confessing Movement had made it clear earlier that it is not asking for "a new definition of faith, but for a new level of integrity in upholding our historic doctrinal standards in a thoughtful, serious, and principled way. We look to our Council of Bishops to assert their traditional doctrinal teaching authority." The unsympathetic response to this call by many of our bishops only illustrates further our theological crisis.

Has United Methodism lost its shared beliefs? We fear so, especially at the leadership level of our church. When we embraced "theological pluralism" in 1972, it was an institutional effort to take our lack of doctrinal consensus, name it and call it a great strength. Though "theological pluralism" is no longer found in our *Discipline,* we are still urged repeatedly to celebrate our diversity. Ironically, the liberal leadership of the church continually asks evangelicals to be tentative in our views and convictions while it remains dogmatic, even belligerent, in its relativism.

When a church loses its shared beliefs, it looks other places for unity. One place the church has sought unity is at the table of dialogue. Unity, we have been told repeatedly, would not be found in our answers, but in our questions, in sharing our experiences and faith journeys. After all, doctrine binds and blinds, we have heard, but experience unites. Dialogue, of course, can bring increased understanding and appreciation of others. However, it will not necessarily bring unity. Why? Because dialogue, if authentic, must still lead participants to some conclusions about basic beliefs. It will not dissolve serious doctrinal differences.

Years ago, John Lawson, then professor of history at Candler School of Theology, made the point that lasting renewal is necessarily linked to theological renewal. He wrote, ". . . while there have been revivals of Christian devotion that have been revivals of simpleminded and unreflective enthusiasm only, the great and constructive revivals always have been revivals of sound, balanced, and scriptural theology, as well as of 'the heart strangely warmed.' *The evangelical renewal of the church cannot arise apart from a renewal of her historic and scriptural evangelical theology* " (emphasis mine, *An Evangelical Faith For Today,* p. 10).

According to its foundational documents, the Confessing Movement appears to be seeking exactly that—theological renewal. It asks no new thing, only that the United Methodist Church be faithful to its own doctrinal standards. Our people have every right to expect that of their church. As the Confessing Movement pursues its missional purposes, Good News will be praying for its every success.

November/December 1996

Can We Recover Our Doctrinal Heritage?

....

"When 'progressive' church leaders use a cafeteria-line approach to church doctrine, leaving behind the miraculous and other hard teachings, it is clear that extrabiblical ideology has taken precedence over biblical authority."

THIRTY years ago this spring the Good News movement was launched by a Methodist pastor in Elgin, Illinois. Charles W. Keysor began publishing *Good News* magazine to rally dispirited evangelicals in the then-Methodist Church.

From the very beginning, Good News' concerns have been, first of all, theological. Whether the focus was on church school literature, confirmation materials, a declining overseas missionary force, or trying to understand "theological pluralism," our chief concern has been for the denomination to rediscover its Wesleyan doctrinal heritage, or in Wesley's words, Scriptural Christianity.

After fifteen years in this United Methodist renewal ministry, I continue to be most surprised by the lack of attention given by United Methodists to historic Christian doctrine. Instead, non-biblical ideologies and special-interest theologies seem to dominate our doing of theology. Mainline Protestants treat theology like a physician who has lost confidence in his medical training and has decided to practice and prescribe medicine by intuition or by what seems popular at the time among other practitioners. Medical exams or state boards seem forgotten. Many just set their own standards.

I am also surprised at how many traditionalists, and even some evangelical clergy, have found safety in the harbor of moderation and the avoidance of controversy. These folks claim to be "mainstreamers" and take pride in avoiding extremism. One wonders how sweeping the revisionist attacks will have to be and how shocking the doctrinal denials ("we don't need folks hanging on crosses and blood dripping," etc.) before some of the centrists will leave the safety of the moderate middle and enter the fray. Far too often career concerns take precedence over principle and doctrinal conviction.

James R. Edwards, a Presbyterian minister and professor at Jamestown College in Jamestown, North Dakota, finds important parallels between our mainline church crisis and the historic Barmen Declaration of 1934, which grew out of the "German church struggle" *(Theology Matters,* Jan./Feb. 1997). Edwards describes two understandings of Christianity reflected in the German struggle. One, represented by the "German Christians," advocated a "positive Christianity" that sought to integrate the gospel as far as possible with the prevailing ideology ushered in by Hitler and National Socialism. They urged the church to adapt to the new thought of the day. The other understanding was expressed by the "Confessing Church," which at Barmen and subsequent synods raised a voice of protest against reformulating Christianity according to Germanic and especially Nazi archetypes.

The lessons to be learned from Barmen are applicable for the mainline churches today, says Edwards, for our struggle is (like theirs) "over the authority of Scripture and creed versus the authority of the alien and humanistic ideologies, between the church's faithfulness to the Lordship of Christ as he is attested to in Scripture versus an accommodation and reformulation of Christianity to the spirit of the age."

When "progressive" church leaders use a cafeteria-line approach to church doctrine, leaving behind the miraculous and other hard teachings, it is clear that extrabiblical ideology has taken precedence over biblical authority. This helps explain why many liberal leaders consistently avoid substantive, right-vs.-wrong kinds of discussions, and gravitate to sharing faith journeys and personal experiences. It explains why many of our United Methodist clergy receive more training in conflict resolution than in systematic theology.

We criticize the German Christians for their accommodation to Hitler. However, we forget that they were simply accommodating Christian thought to the prevailing cultural norms of their day. And we are doing the same thing today, says Anglican theologian Alister E. McGrath: "To allow our ideas and values to become controlled by anything or anyone other than the self-revelation of God in Scripture is to adopt an ideology rather than a theology; it is to become controlled by ideas and values whose origins lie outside the Christian tradition."

When biblical authority is rejected, some other authority inevitably is substituted for it. Not only do we have alien ideologies to deal with as United Methodists, we also have wildly distorted caricatures of true scriptural authority that leave it so misrepresented and unappealing that it hardly survives as a credible option.

Whether we can recover our United Methodist doctrinal heritage remains to be seen. Our declining denominational statistics reflect a sagging interest in our doctrinal accommodations and even less interest in paying for them. By trivializing the substance of the gospel, someone has observed, mainline theologians are making themselves irrelevant, if not obsolete.

May/June 1997

The Irreplaceable Need for Sound Doctrine

. . . .

"With Gaia, goddesses, and New Age fare,
has the church ever been in greater need of
sound teaching?"

THE United Methodist Church is on the verge of giving some much-needed attention to doctrinal matters. The 1996 General Conference directed the General Commission on Christian Unity and Interreligious Concerns (GCCUIC) to initiate a theological dialogue during this quadrennium. Twenty participants, ten from each side of the theological aisle, will meet twice. The first session was in Nashville in late November (only a few days after our deadline for this issue). The second session is set for February in Dallas.

On a smaller scale, another debate took place in September at the Perkins School of Theology in Dallas. Dr. Leicester Longden, pastor in Lansing, Michigan, and chair of the Theological Commission of the Confessing Movement, debated Dr. John Swomley, professor emeritus of Christian ethics at St. Paul School of Theology. Longden took the affirmative, Swomley the negative on the question, "Is the United Methodist Church a Confessional Church?"

Portions of the debate were published in the Perkins *Perspective*; they provide helpful insights into the yawning chasm that divides conservative and liberal United Methodists.

Dr. Longden reminded Perkins students that the Confessing Movement was challenging all United Methodists "to engage ourselves in a serious retrieval of our doctrinal and confessional heritage." He said he agrees with the movement's Confessional Statement that "the United Methodist Church is now incapable of confessing with one voice" that Jesus Christ is Son, Savior, and Lord. When speaking of United Methodist doctrine, Longden means that doctrine which "has been legislatively established in our church by General Conference action and is protected by the First Restrictive Rule of our Constitution." He goes on to assert that while United Methodism is not confessional in the sense of having a central Creed or Confession that specifically defines us such as the Westminster Confession, we do have doctrinal accountability at every level of the church—in baptism, membership, and ordination vows as well as in the job description of our bishops.

Dr. Swomley disagrees vehemently with the Confessing Movement. He sees it as attempting "to systematize God and bolt down our faith to make it immovable." The movement is an attempt "to imprison us in the exclusive dogma" of its members. He insists, "Never in the Wesleyan tradition is the identity of Methodists defined by right doctrine; it is defined by right living." Swomley learned early that "people in the churches that recited the Apostles' Creed and those who believed they were saved by their beliefs actually were concentrating on the sins of sex or drunkenness." They didn't concern themselves "with the larger sins of militarism, imperialism, war, racism and forced unemployment." For Prof. Swomley, "Protestant recitation of creeds, including mere talk about justification or salvation, ideologically functions to maintain a social system that—when it does not engage as Wesley did in social holiness—kills, oppresses, and exploits living human beings."

One can scarcely imagine two more differing views of the place and purpose of creed, confession and doctrine than in the above remarks, though summarized all too briefly.

Two things need to be said about the role of doctrine and creed in the church's life. First, in creed and doctrine, we have the carefully worded teachings of what it is Christians have always believed. As Prof. I. Howard Marshall reminds us, "Christian theology . . . has a normative or binding quality. It is not simply a descriptive statement of what Christians believe; it expresses what Christians *ought* to believe on the basis of God's revelation" (emphasis the author's).

The danger for United Methodism, with our years of subordinating doctrine to experience (and to almost everything else), is that without the substance of the creeds and our rich doctrinal heritage, we are in danger of becoming little more than a religious expression of the Red Cross or the United Nations. "Inattention to doctrine," says Alister McGrath of Oxford University, "robs the Church of her reason for existence and opens the way to enslavement and oppression by the world." Without sound doctrine, we will no longer be the Body of Christ urging the peoples of the world to be "reconciled to God."

Second, fidelity to the doctrines and creeds of the apostolic faith will keep the church from falling into error. With Gaia, goddesses, and New Age fare, has the church ever been in greater need of sound teaching? In recent years, evangelicals have suspected that a number of United Methodist leaders have avoided the creeds and doctrines of the church because they have ceased believing in their substance.

Alister McGrath, I believe, has it right. "A Church that despises or neglects doctrine comes perilously close to losing its reason for existence and may simply lapse into a comfortable conformity with the world."

Unfortunately, that sounds too much like United Methodism today.

January/February 1998

Two

Liberalism and United Methodist Thought

The Devastating Legacy of Liberalism

....

"An important characteristic of liberalism's tenets was that they were primarily negations—that is, statements of what liberalism disbelieved about traditional orthodoxy. Liberalism almost always defined itself over against historic Christianity."

RECENTLY a pastor wrote in a conference paper a defense of United Methodism's being a "liberal" denomination. He insisted the "L-word" was not bad. For support he cited Webster's Dictionary which defined liberal as "generous, openhanded, broad-minded, etc."

Such shallow thinking compels us to look again at theological liberalism to see where it came from, what it affirms and what it does not affirm. Most certainly, the presuppositions and principles of liberalism are still present in United Methodism.

Most laity have little interest in liberal theology. When they hear modern brands of liberalism preached they are likely to respond kindly, "That sermon was profound. I'm not sure I understood it though. It was over my head. Our pastor's sermons are deep."

But if the last three decades have shown the mainline churches anything, it is the bankruptcy of theological liberalism. Realizing this will be an important key to mainline church renewal.

THE ROOTS OF LIBERAL FAITH

Liberalism began to move upon the American church scene around 1880. It brought sweeping changes to Christian churches in America during the first third of the 20th century—a period when a tide of secular thought was flooding in upon traditional American ideas.

Theological liberalism was the religious system which blended with the late-19th-century new scientific worldview. The new science claimed all events could be explained by universal laws of cause and effect, leaving no place for unique events or divine revelation. All data should be subjected to empirical tests for verification, it insisted.

Liberalism was essentially, then, the movement which accommodated the Christian faith to anti-supernatural axioms.

The first step in accommodation was to qualify certain doctrines. Harvard dean Willard Sperry characterized liberalism as the "Yes, but" religion. It would say, *"Yes,* I believe in the deity of Christ, *but* the language of Chalcedon has become meaningless. We must redefine the doctrine so as to make it intelligible to us who live in the 20th century. *Yes,* I believe in the Virgin Birth of Christ, *but* by that I mean. . . ." And on it would go.

While denying tenets basic to historic Christianity, liberalism believed itself to be helping *preserve* traditional Christianity by making it relevant for modern man. Kenneth Kantzer said religious liberalism was an attempt to update "an old and beloved religion so it could survive in the modern world."

BASIC TENETS OF THEOLOGICAL LIBERALISM

During the first third of this century, liberalism clashed head-on with evangelicalism. We see why when we consider the basic tenets of liberal faith:

1. God's character is one of pure benevolence—without wrath. All persons are his children, and sin separates no one from his love.

2. There is a divine spark in every man and woman. All persons, therefore, are good at heart and need only encouragement and nurture to allow their natural goodness to express itself.

3. Jesus Christ is Savior only in the sense that he is our perfect teacher and example. He was not divine in any unique sense. He was not born of a virgin, did not work miracles and did not rise from the dead.

4. Just as Christ differs from other men only comparatively, not absolutely, neither does Christianity differ from other religions. It is just most prevalent among the world religions, all of which stem from the same basic source. Thus, missions should not aim to convert but rather to promote a cross-fertilization of ideas for mutual enrichment.

5. The Bible is not a divine record of revelation, but a human record of the religious experiences of a nation. Thus few doctrinal statements or creeds are essential to Christianity. The only things unchanging about the Christian message are its moral and ethical teachings.

LIBERALISM IS A NEGATION OF ORTHODOXY

An important characteristic of liberalism's tenets was that they were primarily negations—that is, statements of what liberalism disbelieved about traditional orthodoxy. Liberalism almost always defined itself *over against historic Christianity*.

Consider the points cited above as negations for a moment. All persons belong to God, with none to be lost. Thus, universalism is affirmed, the need for salvation *denied*. Men and women are basically good, not sinful (original sin *denied*). Jesus was only a man like other men and did not atone for our sins (Christ's Virgin Birth, atonement, deity and Resurrection *denied*). Christianity is not unique, but just a bit more developed than other religions (church's missionary mandate *denied*). And the Bible is only a human record, not the revealed Word of God (authority of Scripture *denied*).

DEVASTATING IMPACT ON AMERICAN CHRISTIANITY

Theological liberalism was euphoric early in this century, for it believed it was riding the new intellectual wave of the future—and it was. It believed it could rid the Christian Church of its restrictive, outdated worldview and help prepare it for a new, golden era.

So as a strategy by well-meaning churchmen, liberalism set out to attract people to Christianity by accommodating the Gospel to the wisdom and worldview of secular, scientific "modern man." It was determined to preserve and strengthen Christianity. Unfortunately, the impact was just the opposite as liberalism devastated the vitality of the Christian Church in America.

J. I. Packer, contemporary Anglican theologian and author, summarized liberalism's disastrous impact upon evangelical faith, saying, "Liberalism swept away entirely the gospel of the supernatural redemption of sinners. . . . It reduced grace to nature, divine revelation to human reflection, faith in Christ to following his example, and receiving new life to turning over a new leaf."

Liberalism was determined to rid Christianity of its supernatural elements (miracles, the Resurrection, etc.) which just might cause a thoughtful inquirer embarrassment. And it succeeded.

What concerns me about all this is how much it sounds like modern-day theology. Students at our denominational colleges and seminaries often report encountering these same negations in their classes. And several years ago our denominational journal ran an article in which the author/theologian recommended we forget the troublesome aspects of Christianity such as Jesus' miracles, deity and Resurrection. The author suggested we focus only on the ethical teachings of Christianity, for they are what is most important. Alas, the present generation stands on the shoulders of the previous one.

A Curious Continued Benevolence

I am amazed at how patient the Church has been toward liberalism and its subsequent offspring. (I realize there have been times of hostility, such as during the Fundamentalist/ Modernist controversy of the 1920s and 1930s.) Of late, however, we seem to have become theological pacifists, no longer shocked or offended by theological distortions regardless of how bizarre they might be. We calmly, benevolently discuss liberalism or its latter-day derivatives as we would the Sermon on the Mount, not realizing that in liberalism, historic Christianity has been gutted.

And while they mean well, those who reduce the faith to make it more acceptable to the modern mind do the Church no service. Liberalism in its various shades is still a shrunken Christianity—the pathetic result of sinful men and women who, in their quests for intellectual autonomy, would make man the measure of all things. Someone has called it a halfway house from faith to unbelief, from Christianity to secularism.

One hears Dorothy Sayers imploring, "You do Christ no honor 'by watering down his personality' so He will not offend. If the mystery of the 'divine drama' of God enfleshed in Christ shocks and offends believers, 'let them be offended.'"

As long as our society is free, we will have those who wish to improve upon Christianity by restructuring it. But let's be sure we know when this is happening.

In the meantime, let us boldly and unapologetically commend God's revealed Word to our unbelieving world. Let's not cower before the scorn of intellectual sophisticates for whom the word of the cross is still a rebuke. Let's be workers "who need not be ashamed," proclaiming the Gospel with no disguises, revisions or scholarly addendums. And let us have the witness of his Spirit so we may, indeed, be preaching "in demonstration of the Spirit and power" (1 Corinthians 2:4, RSV).

November/December 1989

Our Crisis of Authority

*"If it's Sophia today, who knows what it
will be tomorrow? The bishops or
someone must provide theological
direction for the church."*

ON December 1, [1989] four Good News representatives made a presentation before the Homosexual Study Task Force which met in Atlanta.

As I returned from Atlanta I had that familiar uneasiness in my stomach—I get it regularly at denominational meetings. It comes from wondering soberly, "Could we United Methodists reach consensus on anything?" At such times I realize that we suffer from *a chronic crisis of authority* within the UM Church.

Over the years we have witnessed this crisis as distressed lay people report their experiences with pastors who don't believe the Scriptures to be God's Word, who insist Jesus is not the divine Son of God, who sneer at personal conversion, who discount the thought of Christ's return, who laugh at the thought of Christ's blood being "shed" for us, who deny the atoning death of our Lord, and who ignore the Bible's claims that we live holy lives.

If these laypersons voice protests to their pastors, they are likely to hear their pastors suggest impatiently, "Why don't you go to another church whose beliefs are more closely aligned to your own?" Sadly, many have.

A LOSS OF AUTHORITY

What has happened to us? We have lost our commitment to the authority of the Word of God.

Dr. John H. Leith, professor at Union Theological Seminary in Richmond, Virginia, addressing a renewal group of United Presbyterians recently, said, "There has never been a lively church which did not firmly believe that the Bible is the Word of God written, that Jesus Christ is the Word of God incarnate, that what God did in Jesus Christ in bearing our sins on the cross and in raising him from the dead is of crucial significance not only for Christians but for all people in the world."

Might we United Methodists get consensus on that? Probably not. Any claim that the Bible is the "Word of God written" is immediately seen as a sign of literalism. But evangelicals have pointed out repeatedly that the Bible as the 'Word of God written" does not mean we interpret it literally or that we believe it was dictated mechanically. It does mean, as Good News said in its *Junaluska Affirmation,* that "These Scriptures are supremely authoritative for the church's teaching, preaching, witness, identifying error, correcting the erring, and training believers for ministry. . . ."

THE GODDESS SOPHIA

This lack of serious commitment to Scripture's authority leaves the United Methodist Church open to about anything. The most recent "anything" is a bit of latter-day fare being presented to United Methodists through the book *Wisdom's Feast: Sophia in Study and Celebration* (Harper & Row, 1986). I say latter day because this word about Sophia has been hidden for nearly 2000 years but is now, finally, being made known to us by three authors, two of whom are United Methodist clergy in the Eastern Pennsylvania Conference.

The book claims that a goddess named Sophia is really at the heart of the Judeo-Christian religious tradition. Sophia is a "real, biblical person, then, a real part of the Jewish and Christian traditions" (p. 10). We learn that "she is a co-creator with the Hebrew God, she is a heavenly queen, she is a messenger from God, and she is God's lover" (p. 28). Supposedly all knowledge of Sophia was suppressed by the "church fathers," and it continues to be suppressed to the present day (p. 11 ff.). Prayers, songs and a eucharist to Sophia are included in the book. This new "feminist spirituality" just recently "discovered" in the Scriptures after so many years has already succeeded in driving some United Methodists out of their church.

The response of several United Methodist leaders, including bishops, to this new "insight" has been to comment about our diversity and openness to new theological insights, and that's about it. All this makes recent comments by Catholic Cardinal Ratzinger more relevant for us United Methodists. Speaking to American Roman Catholic archbishops last March, Ratzinger noted that bishops are not on good biblical grounds when they serve simply as "moderators" who are not allowed to say anything definite about the content of the faith.

TRUTH WORTH SUFFERING FOR

Ratzinger lamented the fact that many of the church's theologians and academicians have adopted the relativist ethos of the present day. And sadly, bishops are failing to challenge that relativism. In fact, he says, the bishops have ceased to preach and are no longer bringing the theologians or the faithful in the church to a point of decision, confronting them with "the authority of the truth."

Ratzinger then says, "It is the hallmark of truth to be worth suffering for." Of course he leaves ample room for "intellectual disputation," but he insists that the faithful have a right to know the truth, to know which theologians are right, which wrong. This kind of authoritative teaching, he asserts, is the job of bishops—*even at the cost of popularity, even "at the cost of martyrdom."*

What the cardinal was alluding to was why there is so little opposition to theological error and moral evil from the leaders of the Christian Church. Why has the Church waged such a feeble battle against those forces challenging the classical issues of faith? These are relevant questions for all United Methodists to ask in a day when some United Methodist clergy are leading their faithful in prayers, songs and a eucharist to Sophia. Let me suggest several reasons why we battle so feebly.

WHY WE BATTLE FEEBLY

. . . .

First, the United Methodist Church is seriously adrift due to its loss of the authoritative base of Scripture. We United Methodists have bought into the relativistic ethos of our day. We have taught and left our members with a smorgasbord idea of Scripture—you may just take what you want, leave the rest. Don't expect our new theological statement to remedy this problem any time soon.

Second, for whatever reasons, our bishops have relinquished their teaching and overseeing responsibilities, which have been picked up by program-board staff and seminary professors. The latter have not been reluctant to assert themselves.

Third, we have no forum built into our present structure to deal seriously with theological investigation. Take liberation theology, for example. We have seen it portrayed as both bane and blessing. It's been around at least 16 years—isn't it time we examined it seriously? Why not have a 3- or 4-day colloquy where our best pastors, theologians and bishops gather to hear well-prepared papers on the subject with time for responses? No *ad hominem* arguments, just substantive and prayerful inquiry. After all, the only thing at stake is the integrity of the gospel we are trying to present to the world.

It's no overstatement to say United Methodism faces a crisis of authority. Too many of our pastors and theologians are just teaching and doing what seems right in their own eyes. And United Methodist bishops choose to comment only periodically about our church's diversity and inclusiveness. In the meantime many of our people are coming to worship looking for bread and are getting stones. They go to Gilead but there is no balm. If we have a gospel to preach, its integrity must be protected. Paul charged Timothy, "Guard the good deposit that was entrusted to you—guard it with the help of the Holy Spirit who lives in us" (2 Timothy 1:14).

If it's Sophia today, who knows what it will be tomorrow? The bishops or *someone* must provide theological direction for the church. If no one does, by the time we get around to having a colloquy seriously investigating doctrinal matters, given the rate of our membership loss the past three decades, it may be able to convene in any nearby telephone booth.

Note: *The above editorial was written in January/February of 1990. A Theological Dialogue was finally held eight years later (one session in November of 1997 and a second in February of 1998), initiated by the General Commission on Christian Unity and Interreligious Concerns. The result was a paper entitled "In Search of Unity," which acknowledged the fact that in matters of our doctrinal and theological understanding, United Methodism has no unity.*

January/February 1990

Time for Demonstration

"The conservative 70 percent of United Methodist laity must awaken to the fact that their church has been hijacked somewhere along the way. That is, a small group has slipped into the cockpit, assumed the controls and is taking those on board to destinations they haven't chosen and to which they have no interest in going. It's a serious betrayal of trust."

IF conservative/evangelical United Methodists were given more to public demonstration, now would be an appropriate time.

Why? Because we have discovered *statistically* what we have known *experientially* for years. That is, the United Methodist Church is basically a conservative denomination being controlled, if not dominated, by a liberal minority.

So says a study published recently by our denomination's General Council on Ministries (GCOM) entitled, "An Analysis of Major Issues Addressed by the 1988 General Conference." [This editorial refers to a *Good News* cover article by staff member at the time, Michael Sigler, who wrote about the GCOM survey which showed that about 70 percent of United Methodist laity hold to conservative beliefs on moral and theological issues. In the Southeastern Jurisdiction, 76 percent of the laity embrace conservative beliefs.]

A sentence in Sigler's cover story says it all: "While theological liberalism continues to dominate the seminaries, boards, agencies . . . UMs at the grassroots clearly are marching to a more conservative tune."

The study shows that on the major issues before the church, laity in the pews and even a majority of the clergy [52 percent] are having views imposed upon them that they neither embrace nor support. A small, efficient, liberal bureaucracy is adept at maintaining control by working the system and controlling the debate. How do these folks do it?

One effective way is by approaching issues by imposing specific verbal and behavioral mandates upon the church. Thus members must be careful to mind their pronouns, language choices and opinions. If one slips up in this new control-speak environment, he or she faces verbal abuse, if not censure.

This, in fact, is how an unrepresentative, elitist ideology can triumph—when its adherents turn it into an etiquette or protocol that all must observe at the risk of being disgraced. And it has happened in our United Methodist Church. Let me give several examples:

- Students at our denominational seminaries are so intimidated by the new God-language being forced on them that many have stopped calling God "Father" and just quietly avoid the issue. Control-speak wins.
- To hold the Bible as one's supreme authority inevitably brings charges of being narrow, fundamentalist, or a biblical literalist.

- Those opposing gay and lesbian life-styles are immediately tagged by a vocal pro-gay constituency as homophobic and reactionary. Control-speak insists that kindness means adopting the pro-gay agenda.
- To balk at the views of radical feminists guarantees one the title of "sexist."

You get the idea. What we have here is not dialogue on these critical issues. Liberals have controlled the debate by framing it in their own terms, or they have prevented conversation altogether. It amounts to an actual *imposing* of liberal/radical ideology upon United Methodist laity, nearly 70 percent of whom say they are "conservative." Indeed, it is time for demonstration.

The conservative 70 percent of United Methodist laity must awaken to the fact that their church has been hijacked somewhere along the way. That is, a relatively small group has slipped into the cockpit, assumed the controls, and is taking those on board to destinations they haven't chosen and to which they have no interest in going. It's a serious betrayal of trust.

Sigler's cover article asks, "Will church leaders translate into their decision-making the values and beliefs of their constituency?" The answer, of course, is no. It won't happen until they are forced to do so by laity who are informed and willing to heed the Spirit. This change will ultimately necessitate new faces in top-level leadership.

Author Sigler asks, "Will lay people become more assertive in demanding that their convictions be represented in the official decisions and policies of the church?" Yes, that has already begun, and the tide will only swell.

United Methodist laity have lost patience with the imbalance in church "study groups" such as the general church Task Force Studying Homosexuality. To have only seven of 27 task force members supporting the church's biblical view insults the intelligence of thoughtful United Methodists and reflects a horribly flawed process.

United Methodist laity have lost patience with leaders who ignore church law on issues such as homosexuality and abortion. For a United Methodist pastor from the Western Jurisdiction to be quoted by the Associated Press saying she performs gay and lesbian "celebrations of union" makes a joke of the efforts of our General Conference delegates.

Sigler asks, "Will conservative lay people, frustrated with leadership that does not represent their values and beliefs, continue to vote with their feet?" Unfortunately, they probably will.

But let the record show this: conservative/evangelical United Methodists consider what's happening in their church on these issues to be unacceptable, threatening the well-being of their church. Increasingly they resent a determined minority imposing unacceptable, often offensive, views upon the majority, who also provide a major portion of church funding. So, yes, look for lay people to become "more assertive and demanding until their convictions are represented in the official decisions and policies of the church."

Liberalism has left United Methodism in a moral and theological malaise. Its legacy is confusion and decline. The age of its domination is over. It's time to declare, "The emperor has no clothes."

November/December 1990

Time to Reappraise Our Seminaries

. . . .

"We would not discount the faithfulness and commitment of many of those teaching at our United Methodist seminaries. At the same time, some of our seminaries today present a spiritual and theological environment which is a threat to evangelical faith."

Two decades ago John Lawson, a gutsy professor at Candler School of Theology in Atlanta, wrote a book about the plight of mainline theological education. In his work, *An Evangelical Faith for Today* (Abingdon, 1972), he charged, "It is common knowledge that some teaching which is regularly, and indeed customarily, given in seminaries is contrary to Scripture, and to the chief planks of the historic Christian faith, and to the doctrinal standards of the responsible Christian denominations."

Lawson wrote as an insider, being a faculty member himself. He mentioned the personal pain he experienced as he counseled students who had found it a "devastating experience to be faced in a seminary with new and ingenious arguments on behalf of unbelief, fortified with an array of scholarship."

Writing with no small personal agony, Lawson charged, "Someday there will have to be a great awakening, a far-reaching repentance and a painful reappraisal"

That time for "repentance and a painful reappraisal" has come.

Two letters in April's *Circuit Rider* [1991], the United Methodist pastors' journal, reminded me of Lawson's concern. The letters were devastating and raised serious questions about what's going on in our United Methodist seminaries.

In one, a graduate from a United Methodist seminary, living in California, described his experience as a disgrace and an abomination. He had been taught that there was no actual Resurrection or Holy Spirit. Our bodies will rot, helping the future growth of trees and flowers, and this constitutes resurrection. He was told Jesus was dead and the Bible was an outdated book. God was not the God of Scripture, but an evolving principle of the universe.

In a second letter, another graduate from a United Methodist seminary, now living in Michigan, wrote about his ministerial training. Amidst a withering eleven-point critique he wrote about "faculty who sang the virtues of lesbian marriage, proclaimed the Scriptures to be an untrustworthy witness, and announced Jesus to be only one limited expression of a 'cosmic Christ.'"

These letters struck a familiar chord with me. Just weeks earlier I had spoken at some length with a recent graduate from a United Methodist seminary who shared his experience with me. Bill (I will call him) now serves a church in the Midwest. But he recalls painfully an unrestrained advocacy for radical feminism at his United Methodist seminary, a "wild" openness to homosexuality including active recruiting of gays and lesbians, and a professor who told him "There is no resurrection of Jesus—it's a myth; it doesn't matter." In one of his classes, this professor told him his evangelical/conservative sources were wrong and gave him a "C" for the course, his worst grade in his seminary career. Bill reported that students at his seminary learn right away never to say "God our *Father*." That, too, will lower your grade. He added wistfully, "We learned that you don't challenge professors. You learn to be a fiction writer." But at least Bill survived. A close friend of his didn't and dropped out of seminary.

Add to this one other recent conversation I had with a bright young man who had to stand up to his pastor in a Bible study about the reliability of Scripture. He discovered that his pastor had entered a United Methodist seminary as an evangelical. But while there he suffered an emotional breakdown and emerged a liberal, having capitulated to the seminary's liberal line.

These reports, and many others like them, compel one to ask what in heaven's name is going on at some, perhaps many, of our United Methodist seminaries. One's initial response is to contact some oversight body such as our University Senate. Then one remembers that this governing body recently ruled that it saw nothing amiss with the Dianic Witchcraft episode during Women's Week at Perkins School of Theology a year ago (1990).

United Methodism needs faithfulness and excellence in its pastoral leadership. But our leaders will be no better than the institutions training them. And that, frankly, is a sobering thought.

We would not discount the faithfulness and commitment of many of those teaching at our denominational seminaries. At the same time, some of our seminaries today present a spiritual and theological environment which is a threat to evangelical faith. Certainly, one's faith must be challenged and tested in order to grow. We have no question about that. But to confront students, in Lawson's words, "with new and ingenious arguments on behalf of unbelief fortified with an array of scholarship," is to jeopardize those students spiritually and betray the trust the church has given to its seminaries. We deserve better.

To forbid students from calling God "Father," under the pretense that we must be "sensitive" to others, is itself grossly *insensitive* and violates the consciences of many seminarians. It's a form of thought-control which smacks more of indoctrination than of graduate-level theological education.

It is, indeed, time for a "far-reaching repentance, and a painful reappraisal." The church has a right to expect seminary faculty to be active believers who embrace without reservation the historic tenets of the Christian faith.

Through its sizable Ministerial Education Fund (MEF) apportionment, United Methodism is investing a whopping $20 million each *year* in theological education [for the 1997–2000 quadrennium, it's more than $27 million a year or in excess of $108 million for the quadrennium]. It's high time to look more carefully at what we're getting for such a major investment of United Methodist dollars.

May/June 1991

Let's Get Honest About Doctrine

"Those who leave classical Christian doctrine usually opt to shelter their revisionist views in the protective cloak of ambiguity. They continue using the familiar terms of orthodoxy, but sadly, there has been, says one observer, an 'evacuation of meaning.'"

LAST January, retired Bishop Louis Schowengerdt [now deceased] told the Council on Evangelism audience that "false ideas" have diluted the church's zeal to save the lost. These defective teachings "totally deny the saving power of Christ," he charged.

That's a disturbing claim! If it's true, the church should be alerted. The Council of Bishops should postpone lesser concerns and appoint a blue-ribbon panel of our best theologians to identify and somehow deal with this crisis of destructive "false ideas."

Why hasn't more been said about these "defective teachings?" Is it because the bishop's claim is an exaggeration? No. It's because those embracing "false ideas," United Methodist pastors and theologians included, often conceal them in the rhetoric of ambiguity. So, we hear verbiage like: "We have entered a new age for theology, a new stage of human consciousness. All the faiths of the world are equally humbled by the relativity of their claims before the unknowable transcendent." It sounds so contemporary, so sophisticated, even "deep."

Prof. R. R. Reno, in the new journal *Pro Ecclesia* (Winter 1993), cites ambiguity as one of the three dogmas of modernity (the other two are inclusivity and relevance). According to Reno, ambiguity says, "Because of the diverse historical character of Christian witness, the partiality of human perception and understanding, and finally, the ultimate mystery of the divine, all the propositions which constitute the core of traditional Christian belief are strictly partial, relative and uncertain . . . In light of this ambiguity, any attitude of conviction or certainty is foolish at best, arrogant and 'imperialistic' at worst." Or, in translation, "I'm unsure of what I believe and proud of it!" So much for the Methodist distinctive of "assurance."

A primary function of the dogma of ambiguity, of course, is to ensure us that because we are uncertain of so much about God and Christian experience, we have no clear standards by which to judge other religions. Thus, all possibilities are equally valid. It's perfect for old-line pluralists who would say that in our various religious traditions, we are groping to apprehend that "transcendent reality," which has different names in the different world religions.

As today's church faces the "whirlwind of theological reinterpretations of traditional Christianity," Reno cites the classical role of confession, creedal affirmation, and doctrinal definition to help sift and separate the true from the false, the wheat from the chaff, right from wrong. "Incompatible alternatives are already upon us," he observes, "and they need to be recognized as such." This means sometimes having to say no.

Dietrich Bonhoeffer, the German pastor/theologian executed by Hitler just before the war ended, realized the need for this kind of specificity. He said, "There can be no creedal confession without saying, 'In the light of Christ, this is true and that is false!'"

Making these distinctions, Bonhoeffer believed, was an essential, not an unloving, thing for Christians to do. In *Christ the Center,* he wrote, "The concept of heresy emerges from the fellowship of the church and not from an absence of love. Only when man does not withhold the truth from his brother, does he deal with him in a brotherly way. If I do not tell him the truth, then I treat him like a heathen. When I speak the truth to one who is of a different opinion from mine, then I offer him the love I owe him."

Reno calls pastors and theologians today to religious honesty and integrity. At a certain point he insists, "We need to be honest with ourselves and others when our choices simply remove us from anything recognizably consistent with the Christian tradition." Honesty should mean being straightforward with one's colleagues about what one no longer believes, and in some situations should mean a change in vocations.

Unfortunately, this seldom happens. Those who leave classical Christian doctrine usually opt to shelter their revisionist views in the protective cloak of ambiguity. They continue using the familiar terms of orthodoxy, but sadly, there has been, says one observer, an "evacuation of meaning." Honest searching, of course, is one thing. Purposeful, calculated concealment is quite another.

The United Methodist Church has a Committee for the Elimination of Institutional Racism. We take the sin of racism seriously, and rightly so. What about a Committee for the Elimination of Institutional Heresy? A start, at least, would be to recognize the problem—unmentioned among United Methodist leaders until Bishop Showengerdt addressed it nine months ago.

September/October 1993

The Passing of the Liberal Consensus

. . . .

"The liberal theological consensus that has dominated mainline Protestantism for the last half century is dying."

THE new year will find United Methodists urged by the Council of Bishops to study doctrine once again. We welcome the endeavor.

A few years ago, the world watched walls crumble in Eastern Europe, bringing an end to an era. I wonder if we aren't witnessing the end of an era in Protestant America.

I am referring to the collapse of the liberal theological consensus within the mainline Protestant churches, a view that was swept in during the early 1900s and has dominated mainline church hierarchies ever since. This theology, wrote Anglican J. I. Packer, "reduced grace to nature, divine revelation to human reflection, faith in Christ to following his example, and receiving new life to turning over a new leaf."

Most United Methodist laity are not fully aware of the impact theological liberalism had on America's Protestant churches, including their own. In 1933, theologian Edwin Lewis raised a strenuous protest about Methodists who were abandoning their confidence in the creeds. He deplored those who were opting for the new Social Creed while admitting they had problems with the Apostles' Creed, including doctrines like the "Virgin Birth" and the "resurrection of the body." Even bishops agreed.

It was this growing liberal dominance and the resulting vacuous theology that led H. Richard Niebuhr to memorably characterize the theology of this period by writing: "A God without wrath brought men without sin into a kingdom without judgment through ministrations of a Christ without a cross" (*The Kingdom of God in America,* p. 194).

Theological liberalism however, with its accompanying "Social Gospel," never received widespread acceptance among Methodists. In *Methodism and Society in the Twentieth Century,* Walter Muelder wrote that the movement "was never a popular movement. Only a minority in the denominations identified themselves with it and many of these were related to theological seminaries, to boards and agencies, or to councils somewhat remote from the . . . local churches" (p. 34). This, of course, helps us understand the gap that remains to this day between leaders and local churches. In reality, liberalism was a "consensus" only among denominational leadership.

As our bishops lead the church in studying doctrine, laity need to fully understand the destructive influence theological liberalism has had on their church.

Today, after a quarter of a century of decline that has included the loss of members, money and morale, a swelling crescendo grows among United Methodists for a return to the *sensus fidelium,* the consensus of the faithful, in the life of our church. This consensus has a long history. It is not up for revision with each new generation. It is not determined by discussion groups and straw votes, but by prayerful fidelity to the apostolic message.

Reports about the ecumenical "Jesus Seminar," where biblical scholars raise colored cards to vote on what portions of the Bible they believe are authentic, leave both clergy and laity aghast at the state of theological studies today. In recent years some theologians have used a disturbing smorgasbord (take-some-leave-some) approach to major Christian doctrine. More recently we see even public denial of the faith. Carl E. Braaten, co-editor of the journal *Pro Ecclesia,* notes that frequently the best-sellers in religion and theology "are driven by passionate hostility to the truths of orthodoxy—the trinitarian and Christological creeds of the general councils—all in the name of one kind of liberation or another."

The legacy of theological liberalism has been to leave mainline Protestantism, including United Methodism, susceptible to serious theological error. More recently, feminist theologies have appeared, some of which make no attempt to justify their teachings with the biblical tradition. They claim new authorities.

Fortunately, mainline Christians are losing patience with this theological approach. *The liberal theological consensus that has dominated mainline Protestantism for the last half century is dying. Mainline Christians are seeing it for what it is—a this-world-only system that denies the revealed nature of historic Christianity.* The liberal message has left its adherents adrift in a sea of relativism, with no reliable instruments to help navigate the dangerous waters. All it offers is a handful of ethical platitudes without transcendent rootage, and the unhelpful counsel to look within our own resources and potential to find strength and meaning.

As United Methodism begins to study its doctrine again, the legacy of theological liberalism is a chapter in our heritage that we cannot ignore.

January/February 1995

It's the Theology, Folks!

"For nearly 30 years I have heard pluralists say that evangelicals must broaden, grow, stretch, deepen, be more open, ad infinitum, *so that our message can become more believable for 'modern man.' Too often, that has meant leaving behind significant portions of orthodox Christian doctrine."*

LAST spring Samuel H. Moffett spoke to a group of Presbyterian evangelicals at their General Assembly in Wichita, Kansas. He nearly titled his address, "It's the Theology, Stupid," but decided on a more gentle, "Have We Lost Our Way?"

Sam Moffett is a son of pioneer Presbyterian missionaries to Korea. He served that church as a missionary to China and then to Korea for 26 years. He is Professor of Ecumenics and Mission, Emeritus, at Princeton Theological Seminary.

This elder statesman's text was the familiar words of Jesus, "I am the way, and the truth, and the life; no one comes to the Father, but by me" (John 14:6). Dr. Moffett wondered sadly whether the mainline churches may not have lost their way theologically. He observed wistfully that there was a time back before the great "theological depression" (onset of liberal theology) when we didn't need to ask why we had missionaries, saying, "It was axiomatic, it was simple . . . and overwhelmingly urgent."

He was speaking of the historic, traditional theology of missions at the heart of the modern missionary movement. Evangelical theology was, quite simply, salvation free for all, but only in Christ.

In a few weeks, United Methodists begin electing delegates who will represent us at the 1996 General Conference in Denver, Colorado. One thousand delegates from around the world will convene with colorful pageantry and exciting worship. They also will struggle for two weeks with reports and legislation that could keep them busy for a month.

A major question is this: Will we United Methodists gather at this official legislative session only to continue in institutional denial about our most critical issue—that is, our defection from historic Christian doctrine?

Delegates at Denver will face mounds of legislation about restructure, a board relocation, shrinking dollars, declining membership, flagging morale, and what might be done to turn things around. But will we face the issue that is so foundational for all others, that is, the question of whether United Methodism may well have lost its way theologically? This issue we refuse to address.

Sam Moffett said about this simple, evangelical theology of missions, "It's not as old-fashioned and outdated as some people think it is. It was my parents' theology. But—and this is important—that same theology is also the theology of the Korean Presbyterian Church today." And he noted, rightly, that it's also the theology of the vast majority of third-world churches.

Then Moffett made a simple, but incredibly powerful statement to that breakfast gathering, almost matter-of-factly: "I must also confess . . . that was the theology that sent me to China, and one of my brothers to inner-city America, and another to India, and still another into medical missions. No. I don't ridicule it." Nor dare we.

Be sure of this: A gospel of equivocation, reductionism, special interests, relativism, syncretism, or universalism was not the motivating force that sent Sam Moffett to Korea or that once sent 2,500 Methodist missionaries in service overseas under our General Board of Global Ministries (GBGM). Today's religious pluralists will tell us, often with considerable erudition, that claiming Jesus Christ as God's only Son and the world's only Savior leads to intolerance, imperialism, triumphalism, racism, sexism, and anti-Semitism.

Fortunately, a new generation of young United Methodist clergy are coming along who aren't persuaded by those claims. Neither are they as easily enticed by arbitrary appeals to "institutional loyalty." A greater loyalty has laid its claim upon them—one of devotion and worship of the Lord Jesus Christ, Mary's Son named Jesus, because he came to save his people from their sins.

For nearly 30 years I have heard pluralists say that evangelicals must broaden, grow, stretch, deepen, be more open, *ad infinitum,* so that our message can become more believable for "modern man." Too often, that has meant leaving behind significant portions of orthodox Christian doctrine. The result is like a fast-moving shell game with no one really sure if there is any doctrinal substance left under *any shell.*

The issue is not whether the Christian faith is useful, but whether or not it's true. Russell Kirk, the distinguished scholar and author, has written: "No man sincerely goes down on his knees to the divine because he has been told that such rituals lead to the beneficial consequences of tolerably honest behavior in commerce. People will conform their actions to the precepts of religion only when they earnestly believe the doctrines of that religion to be true."

The question for United Methodists as we elect delegates soon and look toward the 1996 General Conference is: "Are these doctrines still true for us as United Methodists?"

May/June 1995

Thinking About Doctrinal Essentials

. . . .

"For decades United Methodism has neglected its doctrinal heritage. In recent years, it did so under the rubric of 'theological pluralism," a term put to rest by the 1988 General Conference."

THE theme for the 1996 General Conference should be welcomed by all United Methodists. "In essentials, unity; in non-essentials, liberty; and in all things, charity." It sounds good. It exudes fairness and balance.

We also should welcome a new volume from Abingdon, *Unity, Liberty, and Charity: Building Bridges Under Icy Waters,* edited by William J. Abraham and Donald E. Messer. It focuses on the above theme and the "liberal" and "evangelical" polarization that divides United Methodism today.

For decades United Methodism has neglected its doctrinal heritage. In recent years, it did so under the rubric of "theological pluralism," a term put to rest by the 1988 General Conference. In 1982 Bishop Jack M. Tuell wrote, "In recent years we have tended to lose sight of that central 'core of doctrine' and have allowed ourselves as United Methodists to dwell on the 'divergent interpretations,' to which we have given the hideous name of 'pluralism.' And sometimes we have talked as though it is our 'pluralism' which holds us together and which is our most distinctive mark! . . . To suggest this is to suggest only chaos and disintegration" *(Interpreter,* March/April 1982). And "chaos and disintegration" is just what we have experienced.

The General Conference theme reminds us that we do, in fact, have *essentials.* And we don't have the liberty to revise or reimagine them. The "liberty" is in the non-essentials.

The term "essentials" is what Bishop Tuell spoke of as a central "core of doctrine." In his *Theological Transition in American Methodism: 1790–1935* (Abingdon), Robert E. Chiles agrees with Methodist scholar Colin Williams in regard to the doctrines Wesley insisted upon at various times in his ministry. These included "original sin, the deity of Christ, the atonement, justification by faith alone, the work of the Holy Spirit (including new birth and holiness) and the Trinity."

According to Chiles and Williams, Wesley saw those six doctrines as essentials, as non-negotiable. They are nothing less than the historic tenets of catholic Christianity through the ages. Remove any one and you have something less than the historic Christian faith.

So it will be good to think once again about essentials. As we engage in this renewed theological endeavor, we might learn from earlier debates. In his new book *Defending the Faith,* D. G. Hart offers a wonderful biography of J. Gresham Machen, the Princeton professor and Presbyterian theologian who defended orthodoxy in the 1920s. It has fascinating parallels and several lessons for us today.

Machen, a respected Princeton scholar, and other evangelical Presbyterians were concerned about the religious modernism of that day. A church commission said that modernism was, indeed, a problem. Modernism held that the Bible was only "traditional literature," that Christ was nothing more than a man filled with the Holy Spirit, that his life and death were merely examples of self-sacrifice, that he "never rose from the dead," and that he would never return to the earth. Sounds familiar. Unfortunately, the commission denied that anyone in the Presbyterian Church back then held those views. This led to Machen's claim that modernists were using orthodox Christian terms in equivocal, deceptive ways. They were, he said, violating the principle of "truthfulness in language." That, too, sounds familiar. In recent days, traditional doctrinal terms are used but with subtly different meanings. And the laity often don't realize it.

Machen was also concerned about the substance of liberal preaching. He critiqued the substance of a printed sermon of Harry Emerson Fosdick, a gifted and popular liberal of his day. Fosdick's response was an angry outburst: "Never in all my ministry have I been treated like this before, and there is no excuse whatever for such a thing's happening." Machen's critique was not vicious, and he became annoyed that liberals so frequently responded with emotional denials rather than by reflective refutation. Those responses soon turned to personal attacks against Machen. How familiar all this sounds to today's conversations. Even the modest call of the Confessing Movement, urging the United Methodist Church to reaffirm Jesus as Son, Savior, and Lord has brought emotional, *ad hominem* attacks rather than substantive theological exchange.

Finally, as Machen and others pressed the evasive liberals about their doctrinal aberrations, Hart notes, the denominational bureaucracies chose sentimentality over principled deliberation. They focused on sincerity, likability, and being a good team player rather than upon doctrinal clarity. "Goodwill, not critical scrutiny" became the best way to resolve church controversy, Hart claims. As conservatives sought biblical fidelity, they were accused of causing suspicion, divisiveness and acrimony in the church. Presbyterians opted for peace and harmony, but did so at the expense of truth.

As we talk together in these days about essentials, let's remember that when the church has to choose between unity or truth, it must always come down on the side of truth.

March/April 1996

Peeling the Doctrinal Onion

. . . .

"As layer after layer is peeled off the doctrinal onion, laity wonder just what remains at the doctrinal core that these leaders can affirm. Recently a United Methodist pastor informed an inquiring lay person that 'diversity is more important than doctrine.'"

WITH each month that passes, United Methodist laity learn a bit more about how some United Methodist leaders handle church doctrine. It's like peeling an onion, and we are finally getting a glimpse of what's at the core.

In mid-January, 15 well-known United Methodist pastors released their "Statement of Conscience" concerning the denomination's position on homosexuality. "Scripture, tradition, reason and experience convince us that 'the practice of homosexuality' is not in itself 'incompatible with Christian teaching,'" the statement reads. What laity are unsure of is what "Scripture and tradition" these pastors have been reading.

Then, just before Christmas, the *Kane County Chronicle* (12/20/96) carried an article about Northern Illinois Bishop C. Joseph Sprague's remarks at a book review program. The bishop, a warm and empathetic person, told hearers he agreed with Marcus J. Borg's *Meeting Jesus Again for the First Time*, that believing in Jesus means giving one's heart to God, not literal belief in events described in the Bible. (All of us should want to give our hearts to God. The question is what role does Jesus of Nazareth play in our doing so.) He added that Jesus was a "religious seeker" who focused on God and not himself as messiah. It was the church that made Jesus a messiah, Sprague said, adding that it's important to separate the historical Jesus from the Jesus presented by the writers of the New Testament.

As layer after layer is peeled off the doctrinal onion, laity wonder just what remains at the doctrinal core that these leaders can affirm. Recently a United Methodist pastor informed an inquiring lay person that "diversity is more important than doctrine."

The above views are difficult for laity to understand. They have not gone to seminary—that remarkable mainline institution that, one has said, has the unique capacity "to make Christian postulants [candidates] into agnostic social workers." Thus laity haven't learned the fine art of revisionism and reductionism. They tend to believe what the Bible says.

On the other hand, seminaries and liberal academia for years have imbibed secular culture, which views truth as socially constructed by various groups in our society. The result is contempt for any notion of objective or revealed truth.

This is why some United Methodists have begun talking about creeds and confessional statements. They believe something must be done to address the crisis of belief within their church that has led to three decades of catastrophic membership decline.

Thomas C. Reeves, in his important new book, *The Empty Church: the Suicide of Liberal Christianity* (The Free Press, 1996), gets to the heart of the doctrinal crisis of the mainline church: "Here we are at the root of things; the submission of liberal Protestantism to a secular gospel rests upon a failure to accept the essentials of the Christian faith. . . . The first and most critical step in halting the slide of the mainline churches is the restoration of their commitment to orthodox theology. Everything else depends upon that."

But laity will press the case and want to know just why some within the mainline denominations stopped believing in the essentials of the gospel. Reeves attributes this loss to the German New Testament scholar Rudolf Bultmann. who had a huge following among American biblical scholars after World War II. According to Reeves, Bultmann claimed that "virtually nothing reliable could be known about Jesus. He rejected the

Virgin Birth and the Resurrection, among other things, as primitive nonsense. The early church, in his view, invented most of the sayings ascribed to Jesus. In 'demythologizing' the New Testament and translating it into 'existential' language, Bultmann sought to make the faith meaningful to modern men and women." More simply, Bultmann suggested Christians stop trying to defend the historicity of Christianity (which can't stand up to scientific scrutiny) and instead take refuge in feelings and personal experience.

That's why today we hear of theologians dismissing our Lord's bodily resurrection but attesting to faith in the "idea" of resurrection. That's why we read of a United Methodist bishop telling book review attendees that he doesn't "believe in every miracle described in the Bible." He believes they are mostly church mythology.

But if the church is a hospital for sinners, then we must be careful that those looking to it for care don't end up with inferior treatment or ineffective and even toxic medicine. The church has always been cautious about the integrity of its practice. And that is why creeds and confessions are so important. They provide boundaries and help clarify the traditional doctrinal claims of the faith, revealing the contrast between orthodoxy and heterodoxy, between true faith and false belief, between true pastoral care and religious quackery.

Many United Methodist leaders resist having to publicly peel their theological onion. The reason, I believe, is that they have an abiding uneasiness about what really remains of their doctrinal core.

March/April 1997

True Stories that Are Not Literally True

· ·

"Orthodox Christianity holds that the crucifixion is not an obstacle *to the Christian message, it (along with the resurrection) is the Christian message."*

JUST days before Christmas last year, the *Kane County Chronicle* carried an article about Northern Illinois Bishop C. Joseph Sprague's review of Marcus J. Borg's *Meeting Jesus Again for the First Time.* Borg is a major player in the highly controversial Jesus Seminar.

Responses to the review have occasioned two articles of clarification by Bishop Sprague in the Northern Illinois edition of the *United Methodist Reporter.* In his most recent column, he noted accusatory and hostile letters he had received and expressed amazement at the "incivility" of some "Christian" attacks. He also admitted that as a public figure, he must "stand the test of fair critiques, knowing that public people have little private space."

We, too, know what hostile and accusatory letters are like. Our exchanges should rise above such attacks. However, serious debate must not automatically be viewed as being hostile and accusatory. Rather, it's a necessary means of clarification about what we do and don't believe, so we can be held accountable in our covenant relationship. For sure, the bishop has raised issues the United Methodist Church must discuss.

The concern about the review of Borg's controversial work is that Bishop Sprague acknowledged at the conclusion of his review that Borg's book is "a very provocative and, *I think, very much on target piece of work"* (emphasis mine).

The following is Borg's reflection of his first mainline seminary New Testament course: "There I learned that the image of

Jesus from my childhood—the popular image of Jesus as the divine savior who knew himself to be the Son of God and who offered up his life for the sins of the world—was not historically true. That, I learned, was not what the historical Jesus was like . . . I learned that the gospels are neither divine documents nor straightforward historical records. They are not divine products inspired directly by God, whose contents therefore are to be believed . . . Nor are they eyewitness accounts written by people who had accompanied Jesus . . . ."

Borg concludes, "My journey from the childhood state of precritical naivete through the critical thinking of adolescence and adulthood now led to hearing John and the Bible as a whole in a state of postcritical naivete—a state in which one can hear these stories as 'true stories' even while knowing that they are not literally true."

We can better understand the great gulf that exists between seminary lecture hall and pew when we hear about "true stories" that "are not literally true." It takes a liberal seminary education to understand that kind of talk. And to speak that way, for that matter.

The responses Bishop Sprague has received no doubt reflect the suspicion that something destructive is being done to the church's message, especially its Christology. Borg presents Jesus as a religious seeker who was made a messiah by the church.

About the crucifixion, Borg writes: "Moreover, this story is very hard to believe. The notion that God's only son came to this planet to offer his life as a sacrifice for the sins of the world, and that God could not forgive us without that having happened, and that we are saved by believing this story, is simply incredible. Taken metaphorically, this story can be very powerful. But taken literally, it is a profound obstacle to accepting the Christian message. To many people, it simply makes no sense, and I think we need to be straightforward about that."

Orthodox Christianity, however, holds that the crucifixion is not an *obstacle* to the Christian message, it (along with the resurrection) *is* the Christian message. As Charles Wesley wrote, "Amazing love! How can it be that thou, my God, shouldst die for me?" Incredible, indeed!

Bishop Sprague raises further questions about his own Christology, saying, "I believe that Jesus was fully human (how else could he be humankind's Savior?), who in his radical and complete trust in and commitment to the God he called 'Abba,' experienced such at-one-momentness with God that he revealed in and through himself the very heart, the essential nature of God. Thus, he was fully God, fully human—not by some trans-human altering of his genetic code, but by relationship with God, Neighbor and Self."

We would ask the bishop several questions. Is the Son a part of the eternal Godhead, that is, the Trinity? Again, were one of us to have "radical and complete trust in and commitment to" God, might we also attain that same "at-one-momentness" with God, thus also revealing "the essential nature of God"? If so, then in what way is Jesus unique?

The bishop tells us, finally, that something is being kept from the rest of the church. At the conclusion of his review, Bishop Sprague admitted, "We who are clergy have done a disservice to the laity for about 100 years. We've feared that if we told the truth about what we learned in seminary, [you laity] couldn't take it."

And what is it he and others have learned in seminary? It appears that what was learned was how to present the stories of the gospels as "true stories" while believing they are not literally true.

July/August 1997

Three

The Erosion of Truth and Disappointments of Dialogue

When Grown Men Tremble

Our Church Specialists—Adamant and Out of Touch

Ideas Still Have Consequences

The New Intolerance

Reflections on the Re-Imagining Debate

Our Difficulty in Dialogue

It's Time to Tell the Truth

United Methodism's Divided House

A Preferential Option for the Truth

The Conversations We Aren't Having

When Grown Men Tremble

....

*"But in some areas today our itinerant
system seems to have become a tool used
by the institution to compel allegiance to
doctrinal views unsupported by
Scripture . . ."*

LAST year when a major appointment was taking place in the church, a pastor serving a sizable congregation called me to express his opinion about it. He disagreed strongly with the proposed course of action and said so. He had relevant information about what was happening, but he insisted I not mention his call and assured me he would do no more about the situation. I remember the fear in his voice as he said, "I'm afraid if my cabinet finds out I've called, it could cost me my career." His apprehension was real and intense.

Similar apprehension is expressed in a letter criticizing the itinerant system in this issue of *Good News*. The writer ended by imploring, "My only fear is that you will print my name and the bishop will send me to live in a parsonage with a dirt floor."

The same feelings surfaced last year when *Good News* surveyed evangelical renewal group leaders across the church. Of the 39 who responded, 14 said United Methodist clergy were fearful about relating to such a group. They feared "career damage," "their next appointment," or "gaining a bad reputation."

The contradiction of these events struck me. I wondered with amazement *what has happened in the life of our church when grown men are made to tremble?* What is it about our system that makes professional persons cower? (*Cower* is an apt word, incidentally, meaning "to shrink and tremble as from someone's anger, threats, or blows.")

ITINERANT SYSTEM MISUSED

As I have read about Methodism's itinerant system, I have sensed that the strong authority of the episcopacy existed to retain control over the itinerant preachers, guaranteeing their continued faithfulness to Wesleyan doctrines. But in some areas today *our itinerant system seems to have become a tool used by the institution to compel allegiance to doctrinal views unsupported by Scripture and social views which do not enjoy support from some United Methodist clergy and many laity.*

Do United Methodist clergy tremble? I fear they do. They tremble because they know that a bishop's power to appoint determines many things: one's location in the conference, the size of one's church, salary, parsonage, status and the possibility of future leadership positions.

Most of us are aware that among some United Methodist leaders certain views are more acceptable than others. For example, in some conferences, it is not kosher (1) to question where apportionment money goes; (2) to challenge the increasing use of controversial God-language in conference worship services; (3) to aggressively oppose abortion-on-demand or the acceptance of homosexual practice; (4) to criticize the liberationist and feminist theologies so popular in our United Methodist seminaries; or (5) to oppose official church pronouncements on issues such as Nicaragua or nuclear arms. Embracing the above viewpoints will not strengthen one's position in our itinerant system, and may in fact jeopardize it.

NOT IN THE MAINSTREAM

Unfortunately, within United Methodism today grown men fear for their next appointments, their places in the annual conferences and what their cabinets' displeasure could mean to their families' well-being. They fear being viewed by a bishop and/or district superintendent as "outside the mainstream of United Methodism." This familiar but non-specific phrase is used frequently to describe pastors who are not lining up with institutional views.

Good News board member Riley Case observed several years ago that this "mainstream" has really become a "backyard trickle." He's right. It has few pockets of support across the church, but has thousands of opponents.

This supposed mainstream is a set of ideas drawn mostly from the dominant themes of liberal higher education in America over the last two decades. Those intellectual currents have found a home in United Methodist colleges and seminaries and among many institutional leaders.

But it is just those themes which Alan Bloom blasted in his national best-seller *The Closing of the American Mind.* Acclaimed by liberals and conservatives alike, Bloom's book charged that American higher education has displaced moral truth with a mixture of "values." It has forsaken reason for the trivial pursuit of "relevance." The result is a perverse new virtue which urges us to "keep an open mind" and be non-judgmental (be good pluralists!). Its new language of "relativism" prevents us from "talking with any conviction about good and evil."

Bloom's critique sounds as if he were describing United Methodist higher education, and this helps explain why evangelicals feel threatened. They reject the relativistic assumptions of today's higher education, and they affirm the givenness of moral truth, absolute values and the need to make careful distinctions between good and evil, right and wrong. Evangelicals reject immediately, for example, the relativism that assigns validity to all the world's religions. They would, rather, insist on the uniqueness of Jesus.

But Bloom notes that something else has happened. The liberal mind, traditionally open, kind and searching, has in recent years become closed, narrow, reactionary and even mean-spirited. This undoubtedly reflects an increasing desperation among adherents of a dwindling worldview. It also helps us understand why mainstreamers insist that seminary students attend a mainline rather than an evangelical seminary. Do they believe the mainline seminary gives a better *theological* education? I think not. But they do know that mainline seminaries are more effective in indoctrinating students with the preferred liberal worldview. Moral philosopher Richard Weaver contends that much liberal higher education is not really interested in *educating* as much as in *conditioning* the young for political purposes according to its own social and political agenda.

This mainline worldview, with its social and political ideology, is fighting for survival. And it is far, far removed from the moral and spiritual absolutes so central to evangelical faith. That, unfortunately, is why grown men and women tremble. They tremble before their seminary professors with whom they disagree, before boards of ordained ministry with whom they are often in conflict and before bishops and cabinets who hold the keys to their professional careers. They tremble because the seminary professors can fail them, the boards of ministry can reject them, and the cabinets can appoint or reappoint them—to churches with parsonages that have dirt floors.

WHAT MUST BE DONE?

How can this deplorable situation be changed? It would be easy to just urge evangelicals to be more courageous. But that would be too simplistic. Luther said he did not tremble before the pope because he had already trembled before God. And God may be calling some to suffer for righteousness' sake. Jesus said that would happen.

But it is wrong for the church to use the itinerancy to compel allegiance, and it would be irresponsible to ignore such misuse.

United Methodism must face squarely its captivity to the secular relativistic values of contemporary higher education. We have hungered so for the approval of academia that we have nearly sold our souls to it. We must repent of this tragic compromise and unfaithfulness. Seeking God's mercy and forgiveness, we must reestablish our commitment to the full authority of Scripture, giving biblical truth precedence over all theological and social fads.

Genuine repentance would result in a new way of dealing with persons in our United Methodist system. We would see more compassion and kindness toward clergy and far fewer power moves that leave persons cowering. We have boasted about being an inclusive and tolerant church. But we have practiced our own brand of virulent *exclusivism and intolerance—* at persons of evangelical persuasion.

Genuine repentance would result in our institutions and cabinet staff positions being opened up to persons unabashedly evangelical in both their *thinking* and their *living*. Evangelical representation on cabinets, board and agency staff and seminary faculties would be in proportion to the evangelical presence within the denomination, not a mere fraction of it.

One would be naive to think this kind of change will come quickly or easily. Persons in positions of institutional power inevitably resist change and will fight, often bitterly and with the resources of their institutions, to retain their positions of privilege. But change must come, and it will.

The question that remains is whether United Methodist leaders, including our bishops, will work to hasten or to hinder that change.

March/April 1989

Our Church Specialists— Adamant and Out of Touch

"Clerics speak for the church but do not represent its people. In fact they often condescendingly consider the laity ill-informed and choose to ignore them."

ONE wonders how the United Methodist Church can continue championing causes so contradictory to its members' wishes.

Richard John Neuhaus recently reminded us that while the Reformation supposedly dealt a death blow to clericalism by restoring the "priesthood of all believers," the problem of clergy dominance keeps returning in new and different forms.

Clericalism refers to the "political influence or power of the clergy." Neuhaus broadens the definition, calling it the problem of a caste of specialists who arrogantly ascribe to themselves "undue authority, that make unwarranted claims to wisdom, even to having a monopoly on understanding the mind of God." Such a division leads to the exclusion of the many gifts of the Spirit present in the people who are the Church.

The clerical mind says to the rest of the church, "We know what's best for the church and how best to use its resources. Trust us (though you may disagree), and continue supporting us."

This mindset was evident a few years ago when a bus load of 39 United Methodists from northern Virginia spent a day at the General Board of Global Ministries (GBGM) offices in New York City discussing concerns about United Methodist funds going to questionable social and political groups (some quite radical). Upon their return the group reported they had been warmly received by staff but had been told, quite cordially, that policies probably would not change.

This mindset was also reflected in Theressa Hoover's remarks in *Time* magazine's article on mainline church decline (May 22, 1989). Evangelical trends will bring little change, Hoover predicted, because "you don't change focus just because constituencies give you trouble. We've taken as much of a beating in the past and never retreated."

One problem with clericalism, says Neuhaus, comes when church leaders act "with indifference or even contempt toward the people who *are* the church." And the clerks in this clericalism need not always be ordained clergy. They may be functional clerics—that is, board and agency staff members.

This clerical indifference toward the church was demonstrated clearly in the April 9, 1989, Abortion Rights Rally in Washington, D.C. According to the April 14 issue of *Newscope,* some 25 directors and staff of our General Board of Church and Society (GBCS) joined in the rally, along with some 2,500 persons from our United Methodist Women and various annual conferences.

And let's make no mistake: Those marching in Washington were not there in behalf of a woman's right to abortion in the "difficult cases" which make up only 2 to 4 percent of the 1.6 million annual abortions. They were marching for the right of individual women to choose whether or not they *desire* an abortion, for whatever reason.

The UM involvement in this national rally seems to reflect that very clericalism which exudes indifference to and perhaps even contempt for church policy and the wishes of church members. Why do I say such a thing?

Since 1972 our United Methodist Social Principles statement on the subject has affirmed, "Our belief in the sanctity of unborn human life makes us reluctant to approve abortion." During a phone conversation with the late Paul Ramsey, the late United Methodist layman and respected ethicist at Princeton University who helped write our Social Principles statement on abortion, he spoke to me about the pain he felt when the statement was amended on the floor of the 1972

General Conference in Atlanta to call for the removal of abortion from the criminal code. Ramsey said it left United Methodists with a schizoid statement that affirmed at once the "sanctity of unborn human life" and then only sentences later, called for the legalization of abortion. Of course, the next year *Roe vs. Wade* was passed, and abortion was legalized.

Our United Methodist *Book of Discipline* has affirmed the "sanctity of unborn human life" since 1972. Among other things, *sanctity* means "the quality of being regarded as sacred; inviolability." And *inviolable* means "not to be violated, profaned or injured." So United Methodists have affirmed for more than 17 years [now 27 years] that unborn human life was "not to be violated, profaned or injured."

It's a beautiful phrase, but it has been sadly neglected as most United Methodist leaders have consistently supported the pro-choice camp. Little wonder Ramsey was grieved when General Conference affirmed support for the "legal option" of abortion. It actually neutralized the "sanctity" phrase.

At the 1984 General Conference, the United Methodist position on abortion was altered again. A social climate producing some 1.6 million abortions a year was causing Christians everywhere to rethink this now-commonplace medical procedure. So the denomination amended its free-standing support for the "legal option of abortion" to read instead, "We recognize tragic conflicts of life with life that may justify abortion, and *in such cases* support the legal option of abortion under proper medical procedures" [italics ours].

Delegates were exhilarated by this change. When an amendment was suggested that we go on record opposing abortion-on-demand, the chairman of the legislative committee told delegates it was unnecessary and would be redundant. Many of us felt we had taken a giant step forward in opposing abortion-on-demand.

But within hours of this change, GBCS staff members began to play down its significance, saying our basic position had not really changed. In the following four years the church did nothing noticeably different regarding its position on abortion, and both the GBCS and the Women's Division of our General Board of Global Ministries (GBGM) remained members of the Religious Coalition for Abortion Rights (now the Religious Coalition for Reproductive Choice).

The 1988 General Conference tightened the Social Principles statement in the *Book of Discipline* still further. It added the strong words, "We cannot affirm abortion as an acceptable means of birth control, and we unconditionally reject it as a means of gender selection." Again, many of us felt we had tightened up our official position as a denomination with those words.

Yet in light of all this, GBCS staff and directors used the church's name and resources to garner support for the 1989 Washington rally for abortion rights. And 2,500 United Methodist Women joined in the march.

These actions verify United Methodist laypersons' claims that actions taken at General Conference don't really matter. They have argued that boards and agencies will do what they want anyway, and they feel their consciences compromised when they are urged to support financially actions they do not agree with morally.

The church should be doing all it can to reverse the tragic abortion climate in America which is tearing at the very fabric of our society. Christians in America are realizing there is something catastrophically wrong with a society that disposes of its unborn.

The abortion issue is just one example of how The United Methodist Church is handicapped by clericalism. Clerics speak for the church but do not represent its people. In fact they often condescendingly consider the laity ill-informed and choose to ignore them. Such non-accountability must end.

I recently reread pastor Dietrich Bonhoeffer's powerful statement from his work *Ethics,* in which he said, "Destruction of the embryo in the mother's womb is a violation of the right to live which God has bestowed upon this nascent life." This

German pastor (who was martyred by Hitler) finds agreement from other giants of our day such as Helmut Thielicke, Albert Outler, Paul Ramsey, C. Everett Koop and Pope John Paul II, all of whom consistently raised their voices on behalf of life.

I am left with one nagging question: Which giants of our day do the clerical specialists cite?

July/August 1989

Ideas Still Have Consequences

"John Dewey's first principle of thought was that there are no eternal truths. One biographer summed up his philosophy: "All is relative, in change or flux, there are no eternal verities and no moral standards.""

FOR more than 100 years, a staple in American grammar school education was *McGuffey's Eclectic Reader*. It sold an incredible 120 million copies! Here is just a sampling from the old *McGuffey's Reader:*

> "If you can induce a community to doubt the genuineness and authenticity of the Scriptures: to question the reality and obligations of religion; to hesitate, undeciding, whether there be any such thing as virtue or vice; whether there be an eternal state of retribution beyond the grave; or whether there exists any such being as God, you have broken down the barriers of moral virtue and hoisted the flood gates of immorality and crime . . . Every bond that holds society together would be ruptured."

Not bad stuff for musty, "old-fashioned" thought. It brings to mind Richard M. Weaver's classic book, *Ideas Have Consequences*. And they surely do. Early in the 20th century, progressive education was introduced by its noted architect John Dewey, a professor at Columbia Teachers College, which trained thousands of teachers. Along with his new methodology came, more importantly, new ideology.

John Dewey's first principle of thought was that there are no eternal truths. One biographer summed up his philosophy: "All is relative, in change or flux, there are no eternal verities and no moral standards."

Have Dewey's ideas had consequences? It appears so.

In 1984 Alan Bloom, professor at the University of Chicago, published a book that topped the *New York Times* bestseller list for six months. His work, *The Closing of the American Mind*, was a scathing critique of liberal higher education in America. Bloom said that America's educational system had replaced moral truth with a "values relativism" that prevents students from talking with any conviction about good and evil, truth or falsehood. It has forsaken "the great moral truths upon which civilization rests," Bloom charged.

Today we call this new way of thinking "values clarification." Dr. D. James Kennedy, well-known Presbyterian minister and author, recently skimmed a values clarification text used in public schools today. In his words we learn from it "that there are no eternal truths which are valid for this generation and succeeding generations, everybody has to find his own values in his own time. Since there is nothing which is right and wrong for everybody, there are no absolutes."

Yes, ideas have had consequences. And they can be devastating. Consider:

- New York City's schools now have a mandatory curriculum, "Children of the Rainbow," which says students *must* be taught to acknowledge the positive aspects of homosexual and lesbian households. Nine-year-olds receive instruction in the mechanics of anal and oral sex and are given storybooks like *Heather Has Two Mommies* and *Daddy's Roommate.*

- *For Kids Only,* a book adopted in a number of New Jersey school districts, directs children to draw a picture of their parents making love and then indicate whether the exercise made them feel foolish, embarrassed, nervous, "horny," or good.

- Another manual used in New York helps students overcome society's irrational prejudice against bestiality (sex with animals). The only concerns were the dangers of poor hygiene.

- *Changing Bodies, Changing Lives,* a widely used sex-ed text, advises, "If you feel your parents are overprotective . . . or if they don't want you to be sexual at all until some distant time, you may feel you have to tune out their voices entirely."

This is only a sampling of sex-ed courses being used in our schools today. They reveal a concerted effort to trivialize sex and empty it of any moral dimension. Such courses are the consequences of Dewey's new idea a few decades ago that "All is relative . . . there are no eternal verities or moral standards."

Social critic Irving Kristol wrote an op-ed piece in the *New York Times* recently that in the current "culture wars" over family values, the left, with its moral relativism, has already won. After all, he says, the left dominates the educational establishment, the entertainment industry, the universities and the media.

If "family values" are to be preserved, Kristol continued, they must be conveyed across generations by families who embrace those values, and they must have the support of a religious community.

Unfortunately, the pervasive and infectious moral relativism of the left also dominates too much of mainline Christianity, including our own United Methodism.

March/April 1993

The New Intolerance

∙ ∙

"The disturbing reality is that United Methodism has been infected by the virus of this 'new intolerance.' United Methodist leaders do not welcome differences of opinion. We affirm diversity but punish non-conformity."

BISHOP L. Bevel Jones III of North Carolina recently cautioned a group of United Methodist Women (UMW) about the "dangers" posed by the "far right political and religious groups" in the nation. He voiced concern that they are "seeking to control government at the state, county, and municipal levels."

That must have played well with the UMW audience, a group that would never be accused of being "far right." Even to think it makes one smile. I also had to smile at the bishop's warning about those "seeking to control government." I remembered the UMW's activism a few years ago in support of the Equal Rights Amendment (ERA), its more recent campaign to block Senate confirmation of Supreme Court Justice Clarence Thomas, and its vigorous support of the Freedom of Choice Act (FOCA), which would legislate a far more permissive abortion policy in America than even *Roe v. Wade.*

The truth is, United Methodist boards and agencies, as well as the Council of Bishops for that matter, have been trying to influence and control government policy for years.

The bishop also warned his UMW audience about "ultra-conservative groups in the mainline denominations that detract from and even disturb the aims and agendas of the parent body." While conceding that disagreement is "natural and necessary," he went on to say, "But disagreement should not issue in dissidence, disparagement, and divisiveness."

Let me make sure I understand this. "Disagreement should not issue in dissidence." *Webster's* says that "dissidence" means "to disagree, dissent." And to "dissent" means "to disagree, think differently, hold a difference of opinion."

What the bishop seems to have said was, "Look, it's o.k. to disagree, just don't let your disagreement issue in holding a difference of opinion." Neither is our disagreement to issue in "disparagement," which means to "discredit" ideas we believe to be faulty, bad, or untrue. (If the bishop meant that we should not "disparage" individuals, we would agree.) But should we not disparage bad ideas or wrong doctrine? Has our pluralism led us to an intellectual democracy in which we can no longer claim one idea superior to another and worth pursuing vigorously?

The bishop's statement, itself, was disparaging of the "ultra-conservative groups in the mainline denominations." Clearly, he does not think they are a good idea. They "detract from and even disturb the aims and agendas of the parent body," he notes.

As many of us reflect on the agendas of the boards and agencies of the "parent body," frankly, many of us are convinced that these very boards and agencies "detract from and even disturb the aims and agendas of the parent body." Lock-step conformity to those agendas has never been a qualification for membership in the United Methodist Church.

The bishop, I fear, reflects the "new intolerance" of our day. And I suspect he probably has Good News partly in mind when he attacks the "ultra-conservative groups in the mainline denominations."

The disturbing reality is that United Methodism has been infected by the virus of this "new intolerance." United Methodist leaders do not welcome differences of opinion. We affirm diversity but punish non-conformity. United Methodism is one of the few bodies I know of where professionally trained people (clergy) are afraid to express their opinions candidly. Many are intimidated to the core by our binding institutional dogma (as compared to theological dogma).

Supreme Court Justice Clarence Thomas wrote recently about the new intolerance that conservative African-Americans face today. It's a new brand of stereotypes and *ad hominem* assaults toward those who dare question current social and cultural fads. Instead of seeing signs on public doors saying, "no coloreds allowed," they are seeing new signs that say, "no non-conforming ideas allowed." About which, Thomas wrote, "This tactic of damning the dissenter by skewering his character, rather than by substantively criticizing his views, occurs while unyielding praise is heaped on those who write, speak, and think the language of the new orthodoxy."

Thomas says the purveyors of the new intolerance justify their claims in the name of fostering "tolerance," "sensitivity" or a "sense of community." But he says that in his experience, "these popular buzz words are merely trotted out as justifications in an attempt to intimidate and silence those who dare to question popular political, social or economic fads." Thomas adds, "Competing ideas and points of view are ignored, and the jugular of the dissenter vengefully slashed at."

"To intimidate and silence." Hmmm. Sounds familiar. This is, too often, the atmosphere evangelicals face in the United Methodist Church. However, this is not the time to allow ourselves to be silenced. The issues have become so critical that evangelicals must face the new intolerance with increased spiritual boldness and courage. What we're up against, it seems, is something we might call ecclesial and doctrinal harassment. For sure, it's the new intolerance.

November/December 1993

Reflections on the Re-Imagining Debate

"Suddenly, an event from which the Women's Division had tried to maintain some distance—'it was an ecumenical event,' 'we were not a sponsor,' 'we did not help in the planning'—is now boldly supported by many United Methodist women in leadership positions, including bishops."

A FRIEND said to me a few weeks ago, "Jim, the women at 'Re-Imagining' should be grateful to Good News. You took what they said there seriously."

Indeed we did. The "Re-Imagining" handbook ritual included this invocation, "We invoke Sophia, Divine Wisdom . . . . Her voice has been silenced too long. Let her speak and bless us throughout these days." That must be taken seriously. And of course, when major tenets of the faith are denied, lesbianism celebrated, and some claim all of this to be a "reformation," the church must take it seriously.

The debate of the past few months has been a microcosm of how the church has responded for two decades to those calling for accountability. It retreats into institutional denial, while attacking those seeking change. Missing in the defense of "Re-Imagining" has been attention to the serious substantive theological issues that must be addressed.

All the while, Good News has been charged with using "inflammatory rhetoric," engaging in "irrational and distorted attacks," and creating a climate of "witch-hunting, name-calling, and fear." Those seeking doctrinal faithfulness within the United Methodist Church have been likened to—are you ready?—Jim Jones of Jonestown, David Koresch and the Branch Davidians, the militant sectarians of Northern Ireland, the Third Reich, and those who burned Joan of Arc at the stake. The use of such violent imagery of slaughter reveals a church running out of intellectual capital. All of these images, by the way, were found in United Methodist publications. Sadly, these kinds of responses aren't new.

Then, on March 8, a major statement was released defending the "Re-Imagining" event, entitled "A Time of Hope—A Time of Threat." The document came from an *ad hoc* group of nine women, including Women's Division theological and spiritual executive J. Ann Craig, ecumenical executive Jeanne Audrey Powers, and Bishop Susan Morrison (Philadelphia Area). The statement was signed by six of our female United Methodist bishops and 830 other women.

The statement says, in part, "Public attacks on the leadership, *theology* and funding of a recent conference call us to speak out" (emphasis mine). Suddenly, an event from which the Women's Division had tried to maintain some distance— "it was an ecumenical event," "we were not a sponsor," "we did not help in the planning"—is now boldly supported by many United Methodist women in leadership positions, including bishops.

There are several points regarding this controversy that need to be clarified. First, those disagreeing with the "Re-Imagining" Conference are not denying women the right to do theology or serve the church in leadership positions. That is a pure smoke screen. In fact, a number of our church's bishops are distressed about the theology and liturgy of "Re-Imagining." Are they denying women the right of full participation in the church? Certainly not.

Second, "A Time of Hope" also recasts the controversy into one of female victimization, diverting attention from the theological issues still begging to be addressed. Our concerns have not been offered in order to "discredit and malign women." What we have done is to protest a gathering that "discredited and maligned" Jesus Christ, foundational Christian doctrine, and the church's moral teaching.

Third, we all deserve to know whether the signatories, by signing the statement, are giving tacit approval to the conference's objectionable theology and liturgy. The fact that six United Methodist bishops signed the document makes this question all the more serious.

At the March 8 press conference at which the statement was released, the Rev. Beryl Ingram-Ward, one of the nine authors of the statement, offered a startling defense of Delores Williams' highly controversial statement: "I don't think we need an atonement at all. . . . I don't think we need folks hanging on crosses and blood dripping and weird stuff." That statement was so offensive, one would expect no further references to it. Not so. The Religious News Service reported from the press conference, "In light of the violence and abuse directed toward women based on their gender, Ingram-Ward questioned serving a 'Father-God' who willfully kills his own child, a reference to Jesus' crucifixion. 'How can we continue to believe a loving Parent would do this when human parents who do this are sent to prison?'"

Well, you can't say we weren't warned. "A Time of Hope" says that understandings of sacrifice, atonement and martyrdom "are being reexamined." In the case of the above remark, atonement is, in fact, *rejected*.

Some might call that "reformation." We see it as an abandonment of the doctrine which is at the very heart of the Christian faith.

May/June 1994

Our Difficulty in Dialogue

. . . .

"Genuine dialogue will not ignore disagreements nor pretend they don't matter. What may be more harmful is to deny that there are any serious disagreements, when we really know there are but we won't face them."

A LETTER published in this issue of *Good News* reminded me of how seldom we get this kind of correspondence: *Dear Colleague, I've been reading your magazine and am challenged by your evangelical and conservative views. While not always agreeing, I find your articles provide a healthy balance for me as I engage the issues facing the church. Thanks.*

This rare kind of letter has reminded me once again that for all our talk about the value and importance of "dialogue," we have so woefully little of it in the United Methodist Church. Why?

For one thing, authentic dialogue is not easy. It includes engaging another's ideas in a thoughtful, sensitive way. It means listening carefully to what another is saying and then responding conceptually and substantively.

It has been my observation that during the past two decades, we have seen little, if any, genuine dialogue take place. After eleven years and 22 separate sessions of dialogue with the leadership of our General Board of Global Ministries (GBGM), United Methodist evangelicals determined (with the help of an inside source) that the dialogue was not really serious but being done only for appeasement.

As we have seen controversies come and go, I have concluded that United Methodism may well be *unable* to engage in genuine dialogue. During various controversies, what we have witnessed is not usually thoughtful interaction, but rather the church's lapsing into the *ad hominem* response, that is, label-ing critics and reformers as being disloyal, reactionary, schis-matic, radical fringe, and on it goes.

One of the hindrances to genuine dialogue is the tendency to rush quickly to agreement, thus obscuring the differences that made dialogue necessary in the first place. Quite frankly, the church seems afraid to admit there *are* any differences. That may belie an even deeper problem: moral and theologi-cal relativism have made dialogue seem unnecessary, even beside the point.

In a recent book about tolerance and Christian thought, author S. D. Gaede observes that "relativism undermines the credibility of any form of orthodox belief . . . Relativism says, 'You have your beliefs and I have mine, and that's just splen-did.' Orthodoxy says, 'Truth exists, whether we believe it or not, and believing falsely is anything but splendid.' The problem is, orthodoxy always appears intolerant in a relativistic culture."

Of course, to affirm that there is such a thing as objective truth means that some ideas are, therefore, false or wrong. But, as Gaede observes, "If everyone's ideas are okay, then no idea is right."

What we have lost in our dialogue is a clear understand-ing of Scripture's authority. Thus, we are guided more force-fully by an intellectual democracy than by the doctrines and the biblical traditions of our church. The problem with this, of course, is that while all persons are created equal, their ideas don't share that same endowment. Some are true, others are false, and the church should help the faithful determine be-tween the two.

This is a difficult role for the church when it has, itself, imbibed the relativism of our contemporary culture. Richard John Neuhaus observes that these modern, relativistic currents have left many in the mainline churches viewing Scripture and tradition as basically a "troublesome treasure of symbolic re-source, to be turned in whatever direction 'meets our needs' . . . Therefore language about God, Christ, and the sacraments may be redesigned and tailored to conform to our sensibilities and felt urgencies." How familiar that sounds.

Genuine dialogue will not ignore disagreements nor pretend they don't matter. What may be more harmful is to deny that there are any serious disagreements, when we really know there are but we won't face them.

Dr. W. Paul Jones, for many years professor at St. Paul School of Theology, wrote several years ago about the impact of seminary on fledgling pastors. They experience in seminary a loss of innocence theologically, and must struggle with the question, "If others knew what I now know, would they still believe?" The result, says Jones, is that from then on the student is left with a life of "bypassing," that is, "the seminarian has three years to learn how to say one thing and be heard to say something quite different." That means a pattern of dishonesty has begun. Language is being used in this case, not to communicate clearly, but rather to obfuscate and detract.

Doctrine defines who we are as a people and what we believe. "Inattention to doctrine," says Oxford professor Alister McGrath, "robs a church of her reason for existence, and opens the way to enslavement and oppression by the world."

It remains to be seen whether we can overcome decades of our neglect of doctrine. Perhaps we are about to begin talking about it once again.

September/October 1994

It's Time to Tell the Truth

"Yes, these United Methodists have the right and freedom to believe non-scriptural, New Age, relativistic, and Eastern teachings. But one cannot, with integrity, call such views Christianity."

MORE than 20 years ago, the *Ohio* magazine ran a cover story entitled, "What Mainline Preachers Aren't Telling Their People." The magazine's cover was a color, rear-view illustration of a pastor standing before his people in his colorful clergy robe, but with one hand behind his back and his fingers crossed. The story quoted pastors who admitted, most anonymously, "I could never tell my people the many things I no longer believe. They would throw me out." Numerous ministers made such admissions.

I have never forgotten that article. It speaks of the dishonesty of persons entering Christian ministry claiming they believe certain things when, in reality, they know they don't. They are living dishonestly. They don't believe the central doctrines of the faith but have become skilled at using ambiguous language so their parishioners don't "find them out." These are *"stealth"* pastors and theologians, skilled in avoiding the theological radar that would get a fix on their real doctrinal commitments. How often I've thought, "It's time these pastors told the truth."

Well, it has happened. In the Winter 1995 issue of *Open Hands,* the pro-gay/lesbian journal of the Reconciling Congregations program, United Methodist pastor Tom Griffith (Crescent Heights United Methodist Church, West Hollywood, Calif.) has written a remarkably candid article entitled, "Three Cheers for Our Evangelical Brothers and Sisters." Why? Because with their concerns for "belief in Scriptures and the normative creeds and confessions of faith of the church," they are calling us liberals to be honest, writes Rev. Griffith, whose church is a "Reconciling Congregation."

"Now it is our turn to get honest," he writes. "Although the creeds of our denominations pay lip service to the idea that Scripture is 'authoritative' and 'sufficient both for faith and for practice,' many of us *have moved far beyond that notion in our theological thinking. We are truly deceiving ourselves— and lying to our evangelical brothers and sisters—when we deny the shift we have made*" (emphasis mine). His candor is admirable.

Griffith continues, "We have moved far beyond the idea that the Bible is exclusively normative and literally authoritative for our faith. . . . Furthermore, few of us retain belief in Christ as the sole way to salvation. We trust that God can work under many other names and in many other forms to save people. Our views have changed over the years and evangelicals know it. At least they have the honesty to call us to honesty."

I am grateful to Pastor Griffith for his forthrightness. Yes, evangelicals have known for years that many liberals believe little of classical Christianity. Many laypeople know it and some have opted for other churches or denominations. Many United Methodist bishops know it and perhaps some share in this new theology. If so, they are probably careful to conceal it in talk about diversity, inclusiveness, new paradigms and sharing faith journeys.

The sad truth is, United Methodists have lived for decades with *systemic dishonesty*. Dr. John Lawson, retired professor of the Candler School of Theology, once observed that many United Methodist pastors commit perjury on the day of their ordination by saying publicly that they believe and will preach certain things they know they don't believe and won't preach. For decades liberal pastors have told evangelicals that we needed to dialogue with them. But they seldom were honest with us about their real agenda. This, of course, was not real dialogue but merely an exercise in evasion to keep evangelicals from being too upset about things.

The irony is that while engaging in this pseudo-dialogue, liberals have continued the useful smokescreen of demeaning evangelicals by caricature and stereotype. You know the litany: *We are rigid, narrow, mean-spirited, exclusive, etc.* More recently, we have been attempting to silence women and people of color from doing "theological exploration." While aware of our own need to "go on to perfection," we now see through this dishonesty. Far better for them to have just said, "Well, yes, you probably are in the apostolic and biblical traditions. But we disagree with you because we no longer believe that stuff." Such honesty would pave the way for *real dialogue.*

Yes, these United Methodists have the right and freedom to believe nonscriptural, New Age, relativistic, and Eastern teachings. But one cannot, with integrity, call such views Christianity.

With his candor, Tom Griffith has done us a great service. It's time for United Methodists to tell the truth. More than 60 times in the four gospels, Jesus prefaced his remarks by saying, "Verily, I say unto you. . . ." Or, as the New International Version translates it, "I tell you the truth. . . ."

Not a bad idea.

July/August 1995

United Methodism's Divided House

. . . .

"After five days and numerous closed-door meetings, the bishops finally released a disappointing statement aimed more at damage control than at giving leadership. Some bishops wanted to make a stronger statement. Unfortunately, they were criticized, even reprimanded, for wanting to do so."

THE call by 15 UM bishops at the 1996 General Conference for the church to change its stance on homosexuality revealed that United Methodism is a divided house. Events of recent years made that increasingly clear. Now it's out in the open.

One result of this unprecedented action is that we became an angry church. A number of United Methodist bishops were angry at being blindsided by the 15 bishops' statement which went to the secular press before being seen by the rest of the Council. Many delegates were angry because they felt betrayed by the action of leaders who are supposed to *uphold* the doctrines and discipline of the church.

Then, many United Methodist clergy and laity are angry because they believe the church has ended up with bishops who seemingly can do or say whatever they wish without ever being held accountable. For example, many United Methodists are aware that the dissident bishops not only acted in contradiction to the church's present stance on homosexuality, but that they also broke General Conference protocol by trying to influence delegates on a controversial issue that would be coming up for a vote. (In addition, the full Council may have violated church law by holding numerous closed-door meetings with the church press barred.) Had any other group so acted, the bishops themselves would probably have denounced them as breaking covenant.

After five days and numerous closed-door meetings, the bishops finally released a disappointing statement aimed more at damage control than at giving leadership. Some bishops wanted to make a stronger statement. Unfortunately, they were criticized by their colleagues, even reprimanded, for wanting to do so.

I am more concerned, however, about the substance of our divisions, not just the process. The fact remains that even after 24 years of thoughtful deliberations, numerous bishops and United Methodist leaders believe homosexual practice should be approved and same-sex covenants permitted by the church. We all need to be reminded that this debate is not about esoteric abstractions. No, lives are being damaged emotionally and spiritually. Young people are being dangerously confused. And worse, people are dying.

Syndicated columnist Thomas Sowell wrote recently that in sports, war or business, you can talk all you want, but if you lose the game, lose the war or go bankrupt, it's usually all over. There are immediate consequences for wrong ideas or actions. He notes that unfortunately, more and more decisions affecting millions of lives are being removed from places where people pay the price for being wrong. The talk is never forced to face reality. When results go wrong one can simply create new talk by clever use of the media or political process—more images, emotions and plausible notions, sweeping earlier failed ideas under the rug. However, Sowell observes, when you have to pay a price for being wrong, you are forced to speak carefully and seek the counsel of those who really know what they are doing.

Sowell continued, "Among the intelligentsia, a half-baked idea can persist for generations . . . because there is usually no decisive test to show whether it is right or wrong." Maybe that's why many church leaders these days avoid speaking about "right and wrong." Instead, all one needs is a few influential persons who give support and any questionable claim can have a long shelf-life.

That brought to mind some of the "half-baked ideas" that United Methodism has lived and declined by across the years. I remember UM leaders announcing years ago, "The day of mass evangelism is over." (Since first hearing that, Billy Graham has had 30 more years of successful mass evangelism.) And how many times have we heard, "The glory of United Methodism is our diversity!" Or again, "The United Methodist Church is not a creedal church." (That was always a useful cloak for doctrinal neglect.) And then we have heard from a bishop and others that "Homosexuality is a mysterious gift of God's grace." We could go on. These are myths we decline by.

Sowell concluded his essay by observing that it is easy to see why people engage in unfounded talk and promote such grandiose policies when they don't have to pay a price for being wrong. He then concludes, "The real question is why the rest of us take them seriously . . . What have we ever gained from listening to these people? What has gotten better?" Good questions.

The 15 dissident bishops, and many others of our national United Methodist leaders, are badly out of step with Scripture and tradition on the homosexual issue. The local churches of United Methodism have grown weary of anecdotal arguments, biased studies and the continued denial of large amounts of (Christian and secular) scholarly research that decimates the claims of the gay agenda.

United Methodism is a divided house. The episcopal address acknowledged that but urged us all to "stay at the Table." Two days later, 15 of our bishops, by their action on homosexuality, left the Table. The next time you hear talk about divisiveness in the church, be sure you remember just who it is that is being divisive.

July/August 1996

A Preferential Option
for the Truth

*"Many church leaders have fully embraced
the relativism of our culture so that any
thought of absolute truth has been
abandoned. Truth has become the construct
of one's group or sub-group. . . . There is no
longer a common or universal reference
point of truth which is used as a guide."*

FOR years we have heard that the church must have a "preferential option for the poor." For certain, when the church has been faithful in any age, it has shown a profound and practical concern for the poor.

However, our concern for the poor can be thwarted by a misunderstood and misguided benevolence about what may actually help the poor. What the church needs, it seems, in this and all its concerns, is "a preferential option for the truth."

The Rev. Paul Stallsworth, president of the pro-life Taskforce of United Methodists on Abortion and Sexuality (TUMAS), wrote in that organization's June newsletter, *Lifewatch,* that the recent General Conference and the church in general have not recently given much attention to the matter of truth. He reminds us that we follow Jesus Christ who is Truth incarnate.

Those words have haunted me in recent weeks. We hear much in church discussions these days about personal experiences, feelings, and faith journeys. We hear woefully little about truth. We hear about consensus-building, little about obeying the truth. Dialogue seems beneficial almost as an end in itself, with little anticipation of discovering truth.

Paul urged Timothy to be a workman "who correctly handles the word of truth" (2 Timothy 2:15). He then reminds

Timothy about two teachers, Hymenaeus and Philetus, "who have wandered away from the truth" and as a result "they destroy the faith of some" (2:18). Mishandling the truth can be destructive to the faith of the Church.

We must never forget that it is the "word of truth" with which the church has been entrusted. What an awesome responsibility for those of us charged with the teaching and the preaching of it!

I was reminded of this again while attending the beautiful service for the consecration of our four new bishops at the conclusion of the North Central Jurisdictional Conference in Fort Wayne, Indiana, on July 19. During the liturgy of consecration, the four newly elected bishops were reminded, "As servants of the whole Church, you are called to preach and teach the truth of the Gospel to all God's people." They were then asked several questions, including, "Will you guard the faith, order, liturgy, doctrine, and discipline of the Church against all that is contrary to God's Word?" Clearly, bishops must "correctly handle the word of truth."

But why has the matter of truth become a problem for the mainline church? Thomas F. Torrance, a Scottish theologian, wrote recently that "by and large . . . little attention is given throughout the Church to the primary truths of the Gospel, for a rejection of belief in the supernatural seems to have set in . . . that discounts God's direct action in revelation and history. As a result people's confidence in the truth and authority of the Holy Scriptures is undermined, and a steady erosion of the Gospel is found in the preaching and teaching of the Church." The result, says Torrance, is that "Christianity is reduced to being not much more than the sentimental religious froth of a popular socialism . . . . What Americans call 'car bumper theologies' replace the distinctive doctrines of the Christian Faith, and trendy substitute-religions replace strong evangelical witness to Jesus Christ as Lord and Savior." Strong words, but accurate.

What has happened to our understanding of truth? For years the mainline church sought to make the gospel "relevant" so that "modern man" might not be embarrassed by its super-natural claims and, thus, more easily believe it.

We have gone beyond that now. Many church leaders have fully embraced the relativism of our culture so that any thought of absolute truth has been abandoned. Truth has become the construct of one's group or sub-group. Each is free to tell its own story or paradigm, but it is "true" only for them. There is no longer a common or universal reference point of truth which is used as a guide. Any such universal claim to truth, these folks say, would be exclusive of all other views, pushing them to the margins, and that would be a form of oppression. Thus, the concept of universal, commonly held, objective truth is rejected for a more inclusive and pluralistic understanding of truth.

This explains, obviously, why much of our dialogue is an exercise in futility, with two sides talking past one another. Evangelicals have a specific understanding of truth. When we say the Apostles' Creed, we don't say, "It was believed by the early church that on the third day he arose from the dead." We say simply, as a matter of historical fact, "on the third day he rose from the dead."

What must be clarified for us right away is whether today's leaders believe the gospel to be revealed truth. Or are they comfortable with what a pastor told a family in his church? "I don't really think it matters," he said, "whether any of these beautiful stories of the Bible describe what actually happened. All that really matters is their transforming power in people's lives."

For our church to be renewed, we need to be sure the story is true. We will need a "preferential option for the truth."

September/October 1996

The Conversations We Aren't Having

. . . .

"These moral and theological issues are of enormous proportions for both our church and civilization . . . . We wonder at the reticence of many United Methodist leaders to discuss openly, debate candidly and urge publicly a renewed fidelity to the great principles of biblical faith and moral truth."

I WAS recently impressed by an essay from Dr. Peter Kreeft, professor of philosophy at Boston College, found in *Reclaiming the Great Tradition* (InterVarsity, 1997). Kreeft depicts a modern Rip van Winkle, having fallen asleep in 1955, awakening to find the United States of 1995 with frightening statistics of moral and cultural decay. Mr. van Winkle would be astounded, as are most Americans today, about the "massive destruction of morality, honesty, safety, families, marriages, trust, the sanctity of life, sex and even belief in objective truth and goodness."

Kreeft asks, "What is the city set on a hill doing about the fact that all the septic tanks on the hill are backing up?" What strikes me about this "massive destruction" is just how little conversation we are having within United Methodism about it all.

One common concern from United Methodist laity is, "Our pastor won't address any of the serious moral problems tearing away at our society." It seems we have re-written the Great Commission today to read, "Go ye into all the world and preach tranquility." We recall the rebellious Israelites who said to the prophets years ago, "Give us no more visions of what is right!

Tell us pleasant things, prophesy illusions . . . and stop confronting us with the Holy One of Israel!" (Isaiah 30:10–11) C'mon Isaiah, be positive!

Kreeft noted the conflict going on within the Roman Catholic Church in America where "dissenters" (he noted they used to be called heretics) control nearly all the theology departments of major universities. The dissent is not about the Nestorian or Docetic or other various heresies first. It is moral before being theological. And within moral theology, the dissenters aren't defending theft, nuclear war, oppression or social injustice. Rather, the dissent is almost always about one thing: sex. "Every one of the specific issues dissenters dissent from concerns *traditional sexual morality versus the sexual revolution*, which the church stubbornly refuses to bless" (emphasis mine).

Kreeft goes on to say that even theological issues like the dating of the Gospels and the facticity of the resurrection are driven by sexual questions. He explains: "If Jesus did not really rise, he is not really God; and if the Gospels were not written by eyewitnesses and do not tell us the words of God incarnate but only the words of a man or . . . 'the early Christian community,' then their authority and those of the church they say Christ founded is undermined. Authority over what?"

These moral and theological issues are of enormous proportions for both our church and civilization. The homosexuality challenge is not a tangential concern. We wonder at the reticence of many United Methodist leaders to discuss openly, debate candidly and urge publicly a renewed fidelity to the great principles of biblical faith and moral truth. It brings to mind the piercing words of Martin Luther: "If I profess with the loudest voice and clearest exposition every portion of the truth of God, except precisely that little point which the world and the devil are at that moment attacking, I am not confessing Christ, however boldly I may be professing Christ."

Some may claim we are having the debate we need on the great issues of the day. I don't believe we are. In 1995 Professor

Tom Oden wrote, *Requiem: A Lament in Three Movements*, published by Abingdon, in which he identified "the failure of contemporary theological education and its accompanying ideology," and called for "a return to classical Christian theological roots and categories." Oden has spent his life in the world of theological education and was fully qualified to share the anguish of his heart about how our seminaries are preparing persons to do ministry. Yet the institutional response was to downplay and refuse to engage the substance of Oden's work.

Others might point to the more recent Theological Dialogues in Nashville and Dallas and claim we are seeing serious interaction. However, one might respond that the most amazing thing about the dialogue is how long it took to happen. Good News was launched in 1967 out of deep concern by a significant segment of the United Methodist Church that we had departed from Scriptural Christianity, our historic Wesleyan theological heritage. More recently, the Confessing Movement was launched expressing concern that the United Methodist church was "in danger of abandoning the gospel." The movement wants to make sure United Methodism can still affirm Jesus Christ "as Son, Savior, and Lord." That would seem important enough. However, the response from many United Methodist leaders has been more one of annoyance—that such theological conversations are a nuisance, that we surely don't need any doctrinal litmus tests.

Kreeft warns that not only has moral practice in America declined, so has moral theory or belief. This is more radical and destructive. The nation that doesn't practice its principles can still be called back to them. "If the road maps are still there, we can find our way back to the road," Kreeft says. But to no longer believe the principles is to burn the maps, making it far less likely we would find our way back. A sobering thought, indeed.

United Methodist evangelicals want to make sure our road maps are still firmly in place today, guiding the church safely through its moral and theological challenges.

September/October 1998

Four

The Homosexuality Controversy and Its Deeper Meaning

Northern Illinois' Sad, Sad Tale

"Any of the above factors could have led to her tragic death. We will never know. But for the bishop to speculate publicly before his annual conference that opposition to her ordination 'added to her decision to end her life' seems unfair and highly irresponsible."

How is it that United Methodists who take a position they believe to be consistent with Scripture and church law end up getting attacked? That's exactly what happened at this spring's session of the Northern Illinois Annual Conference. It's disturbing.

For several years that conference was embroiled in controversy over known lesbian Phyllis Jean Athey's candidacy for the ordained ministry. A member of the Wheadon United Methodist Church in Evanston, she was held up in her ordination process in 1987 due to a questionable vote from her District Committee on Ministry. However, a Judicial Council ruling cleared the way for her to be ordained deacon at the 1988 annual conference,

A number of pastors in the conference were aware of her lifestyle. Those opposing her candidacy on the grounds of her sexual preferences had learned that Phyllis and Mary Jo Osterman had been united in a lesbian covenanting service at the Wheadon United Methodist Church in 1982. The actual liturgy used in that service, names included, is found in a book by Rosemary Ruether, a teacher at Garrett-Evangelical Theological Seminary, entitled *WomenChurch: Theology and Practice of Feminist Liturgical Communities* (Harper, 1985). They had also discovered that Phyllis and Mary Jo had co-authored *The Lesbian Relationship Handbook,* published by Kinheart (an organization funded partially by the conference), 1984. In the introduction to the book, the authors acknowledged their lesbian relationship.

A CONFUSING TRAGEDY

By early spring of this year, evangelicals aware of Athey's lifestyle were trying to prevent her approval as a deacon. But in March, to the surprise of almost everyone, Phyllis announced she would not seek ordination, and she moved from Evanston back to her parents' home in Holland, Michigan.

Tragically, on May 23 Phyllis died there of a self-inflicted gunshot wound. A letter from the Northern Illinois Cabinet dated May 25 told pastors and others of her death. The letter acknowledged Phyllis had been a certified candidate for ordained ministry in the conference. It said, "Her deep faith and personal integrity did not allow her to compromise on her witness to the inclusive nature of ministry." In an apparent jab at those opposing her ordination, it went on, "While we do not know all the factors which led to her death, we acknowledge the extreme pressure and conflict gay men and lesbians live under in church and society. We confess our own participation in causing the pain and isolation they experience."

IRRESPONSIBLE SPECULATIONS

The June 24 supplement of the Northern Illinois Conference edition of the *United Methodist Reporter* tells the disturbing story of anger and recrimination expressed toward those who, in allegiance to Scripture and church law, had opposed Phyllis' candidacy.

Bishop Jesse R. DeWitt, in his final address as bishop in the Chicago area, was critical of those who had supposedly broken confidences about Athey's lifestyle—a curious charge since almost all the information concerning Phyllis' sexual orientation was found in published material.

In a low blow which would seemingly direct the deep hurt and anger over Phyllis' death toward evangelicals, the bishop said, "Some believe the assault on Phyllis Athey by this conference added to her decision to end her life." And his call for persons in the conference "to use appropriate channels for calling individuals into question" seems to be a chilling call for reprisals against members of the conference who opposed the Athey candidacy.

This charge was unwise and unfair. Numerous other factors must be considered in the painful complexity of Phyllis' suicide. These would include reports of a broken relationship with Mary Jo, her father's serious illness, and the widely recognized instability of homosexual relationships. Clinical evidence reveals, according to Armand M. Nicholi II, Director of Student Health Services at Harvard, that these relationships are "increasingly lonely and frustrating, regardless of how permissive and accepting our society becomes."

Any of the above factors could have led to her tragic death. We will never know. But for the bishop to speculate publicly before his annual conference that opposition to her ordination "added to her decision to end her life" seems unfair and highly irresponsible.

FUNDING GAY CENTER

Anger surfaced again during debate over proposed legislation calling on the Northern Illinois Conference to ban funding of homosexual caucuses or groups or "otherwise using such funds to promote the acceptance of homosexuality." This was an effort to apply the national funding prohibition of Par. 906.13 of the *Discipline* to annual conference boards, agencies and groups.

The proposed legislation came from the Administrative Board of Calvary United Methodist Church in Chicago. It focused on the conference Board of Church and Society's funding of Kinheart Women's Center in Evanston, described by the *Reporter* article as a "center for lesbians, gay men, their families and friends." While some claim the center is only for ministry and counseling of homosexual persons and their families, others believe it goes beyond ministry and includes advocacy and support of homosexual practice as an acceptable lifestyle.

During the heated debate a ministerial member angrily criticized the proposal to cut off funding, saying, "I think this document needs to be castigated publicly." He compared the authors of the legislation to the Romans at the time of Christ's crucifixion. A member of Calvary United Methodist Church, sponsor of the legislation, asked for an apology for that "slur." And when the bishop was asked to offer a prayer of reconciliation, he did so only after saying, "An attack upon one is an attack upon all." It would appear that persons supporting valid legislative proposals were being portrayed as attackers of others in the conference.

"I HAVE BEEN SHOCKED"

Numerous times during the annual conference plenary sessions, conference leaders referred to the "sin of homophobia." And Rev. Betty Jo Birkhahn-Rommelfanger, pastor of the Wheadon congregation, said during the annual conference's memorial service address, "I have been shocked at the way Phyllis was dehumanized and treated unjustly. She, like others of our brothers and sisters who are gay and lesbian, was scorned and ridiculed and denied her full humanness by society, family and the church. I really believe that we would not have let her be so ill-treated and denied ordination with such silence and confusion had she not been a lesbian." She also spoke of the fear, hatred and prejudice of Northern Illinois Conference congregations toward lesbians and gay men.

HALTING VINDICTIVENESS

This kind of recrimination on the floor of a United Methodist annual conference is indefensible. Some United Methodists may be afflicted with homophobia—an inordinate fear of homosexual persons. But be sure of this—many United Methodists who are unequivocally opposed to homosexual practice are thoughtful, mature Christians who have prayerfully and deliberately studied the matter at length and have concluded that homosexual practice is not the will of God for humankind. United Methodist delegates at General Conference in St. Louis recently reaffirmed this conviction with a number of strong votes following a high-caliber debate. *Isn't it time we began to implement this standard at every level of our church life?* And isn't it time to end the vindictiveness toward those urging the church to do so?

A number of persons left the Northern Illinois Annual Conference session in June feeling personally attacked by their conference leadership—attacked because they took a conscientious stand they believed was consistent with Scripture and church law. What's so disturbing is that those persons embracing the church's present official position on homosexuality were made to feel disloyal, unloving and in serious error. Some pastors are already questioning the future of their ministry in that conference, given the anger they felt from conference leaders. This was a sad, sad chapter in the life of our church.

United Methodism cannot afford another quadrennium of winking at or ignoring the clear, carefully stated standards of the church on this issue. Our bishops should require and expect adherence to church standards at every level of our annual conferences and national structure. And by all means they should disallow any mean-spiritedness toward those who urge faithfulness to these standards.

September/October 1988

Is the Homosexuality Task Force Biased?

". . . we believe a task force undertaking such an in-depth study should contain a majority of persons who support the church's historic, scriptural stand on the matter."

THE church has established its task force to conduct the four-year study of homosexuality authorized by the 1988 General Conference. But the makeup of the task force leaves many of us feeling anxious about the matter and ready to raise a voice of protest.

In our special report on General Conference, *Good News* (May/June 1988) voiced little apprehension about the proposed four-year study of homosexuality—a study intended to be fair and far-reaching in its biblical, theological and scientific inquiry. We believed the committee would be representative of the entire church.

Overall, we had been encouraged by the delegates' actions in St. Louis on the issue of homosexuality. The conference spoke decisively in numerous major votes, affirming that United Methodism's present standards in the *Discipline* should not be changed. By a strong 80–20 percent vote, delegates retained a slightly altered Social Principles statement which insists the practice of homosexuality is "incompatible with Christian teaching."

We also editorialized confidently that "the church will look carefully at who is appointed" to the study committee. We warned that "objective task forces can easily be manipulated to become an advocacy forum." But we did not believe it would happen.

For one thing, any such advocacy would violate paragraph 906.12 of the *Discipline* which prohibits church funds being used for homosexual advocacy. Bishop Richard Looney, who chaired the General Conference legislative subcommittee dealing with the homosexuality study, spoke to that issue on the floor of the conference, saying, ". . . this [homosexuality study] is not an advocacy proposal . . . this is a study proposal. And it's very carefully spelled out that this is to be a balanced presentation. . . ." (*Daily Christian Advocate,* May 4, 1988, p. 456). The key word is *balanced.*

We have looked carefully at the task force named by the General Council on Ministries (GCOM) in November, and we don't like what we see. We would not describe the task force as either balanced or genuinely representative of the United Methodist Church. We are distressed by the group's makeup and feel betrayed by its imbalance.

The group will conduct a study on this critical issue during the next four years, spending nearly $200,000 in the process. Its purpose: to analyze the problem of homosexuality theologically and ethically and, more importantly, to "explore the implications of its study for the Social Principles." That means the task force could take a proposal to the 1992 General Conference asking delegates to remove the statement in the Social Principles which now affirms that the practice of homosexuality is "incompatible with Christian teaching."

Such action would be devastating to the well-being of our denomination. It would most certainly cause a major split within the church. This only adds to the critical importance of the makeup of this group.

Therefore, we must note several reservations about the task force. First, from what we know thus far about the members, we are not sure whether a majority of the group supports the church's present stand on homosexuality. If a majority of the study group does *not* support the church's present stand, the whole enterprise is flawed by a serious imbalance from the start.

Granted, all committee members will bring their prior convictions with them; no one comes to the task with total objectivity. Still, we believe a task force undertaking such an in-depth study should contain a majority of persons who support the church's historic, scriptural stand on the matter. Recognizing that diversity is important, is this task force's diversity *proportionate* (1) to the views expressed by delegates in St. Louis and (2) to the views held by the church's members? We think not.

To illustrate our concern, let's look more closely at the makeup of the task force. The committee has two persons representing the gay community. One is a pastor of a "reconciling congregation" from Minneapolis, and the other is a lesbian from Sacramento, California. (Reportedly, no homosexual male could be found who would participate, so a pastor of a "reconciling congregation" was chosen.)

Sally Geis from Colorado, another task force member, strongly supported homosexual minister Julian Rush when he was investigated by the Rocky Mountain Annual Conference.

The writings of Rebecca Parker from Washington state (another member of the task force) challenge traditional doctrines such as original sin, salvation and the Atonement. This leaves us doubtful that she will affirm the church's traditional standards. After further inquiry, we are unsure of the views of Tex Sample, Arthur Pressley, Victor Furnish, and Bruce Hilton.

Based on our research, perhaps only eight to ten of the 26 members of this task force would affirm the church's present standards on homosexuality. We would love to discover otherwise. In light of the 80–20 percent vote by delegates last May, United Methodists have a right to expect *at least* a clear majority of the task force members to support the church's standards.

A second problem with the task force is that at least seven of the 26 members are faculty or staff members of a United Methodist seminary. Our seminaries, for the most part, are United Methodism's most unrepresentative institutions and are often out of touch with local church members.

An additional problem with the seminary representation is that the task force has no *orthodox* biblical scholar—i.e., Old or New Testament specialist—as a member. This is a glaring omission for a group planning long-term study of the *biblical,* theological and scientific questions related to homosexuality.

A third problem with the task force is that it is not representative of United Methodist membership by jurisdiction. For example, the Western Jurisdiction, by far the least populous in membership, has six members on the task force. However, the more populous North Central and South Central Jurisdictions are each represented by only four persons. This is significant when we realize that the Western Jurisdiction is clearly United Methodism's most liberal on both theological and social issues. Interestingly, the task force's chairperson comes from the Western Jurisdiction.

Finally, we have a problem with the fact that, by design, two persons representing the gay community were invited to be members of the task force. Although it was charged to conduct an "objective study" of homosexuality, the task force's objectivity seems compromised from the start. But having already appointed these two, the committee should balance their presence by including two ex-gays—that is, persons who have participated in the homosexual lifestyle but are, by God's grace, no longer involved.

Exodus International lists some 50 ministries in 26 different states where persons are being liberated from the gay lifestyle. Ex-gays are ready to witness to the redeeming, transforming grace of Christ that has freed them. If the church is serious about seeing lives transformed by God's grace, why would not ex-gays be included in such a study?

In summary, we fear that the task force authorized by the 1988 General Conference to conduct a four-year, balanced and in-depth study of homosexuality is biased toward views not consistent with those presently stated in our *Discipline.* We hope we are proven wrong, but we must express strong reservations about what this could mean for the total work of the task force.

Perhaps it is not too late to rectify the situation. The full steps toward correcting the imbalance might be (1) adding several orthodox, biblical scholars (Old and New Testament specialists); (2) adding additional persons to correct the group's geographic imbalance and (3) adding two ex-gays to the group.

Also, to inform the church about the task force's mindset, the group should poll its members at its first orientation meeting to determine what its *predisposition* is toward the church's present standards on homosexuality. More specifically, we need to know how many committee members *have been and remain* supportive of the present ban against the ordination of self-avowed practicing homosexuals and of the statement in the Social Principles that the practice of homosexuality "is incompatible with Christian teaching."

The entire church has a right to know the results of such a poll as the task force begins its work.

January/February 1989

Task Force Ignores Scriptural Standard

· ·

"Evangelicals are not distressed about this because they are homophobic. They are distressed by the likelihood that if church leaders can't find an authoritative word from Scripture about homosexual practice, they probably can't find an authoritative word about anything."

THE Homosexuality Study Task Force voted 17–4 to recommend *removing* from the Social Principles of our *Book of Discipline* the claim that homosexual practice "is incompatible with Christian teaching."

The new wording in the *Discipline* would claim "that the church has been unable to arrive at a common mind on the compatibility of homosexual practice with Christian faith." As its example it says, "Many consider this practice incompatible with Christian teaching. [But] many believe it acceptable when practiced in a context of human caring and covenantal faithfulness."

In addition, the new statement claims, "The present state of knowledge in the relevant disciplines does not provide a satisfactory basis upon which the church can responsibly maintain a specific prohibition of homosexual practice." So the "incompatible with Christian teaching" phrase, which has served us well for 19 years, should be dropped.

In official action the Good News Executive Committee voiced "grave concern" about the committee's recommendation, calling it divisive and unbiblical and charging that it reflects a flawed process because of the biased makeup of the study committee from the start. In fact, *Good News* editorialized about the committee's imbalance just weeks after its members were announced.

While the task force's action was not a surprise to us, it is nonetheless deeply distressing and will offend a large segment of the United Methodist Church. The committee made several highly questionable claims.

First, we are amazed at the committee's claim that "the church has been unable to arrive at a common mind on the compatibility of homosexual practice with Christian faith." As recently as the 1988 General Conference, delegates voted 80 percent to 20 percent to *affirm* the very statement the committee wants to remove. To us, that is a "common mind" among United Methodists that homosexual practice is "incompatible with Christian teaching."

Then, another surprising claim came from the Rev. J. Philip Wogaman, professor at Wesley Theological Seminary [now senior minister at Foundry United Methodist Church in Washington, D.C.] and lead writer for the recommendation. Wogaman told the committee the change is meant as a compromise and is unlikely to please those on either side of the issue. But as committee member, Bishop Richard Looney (South Georgia), said to the *Wesleyan Christian Advocate,* "Taking out the passage that says homosexuality is incompatible with Christian teaching is not a compromise, but a changing of the church's strongly held position."

The church has battled to retain the "incompatible" phrase in the Social Principles at the last four general conferences. One wonders how this recommendation could possibly be seen as a compromise.

Perhaps the most devastating aspect of the committee's action is that it reflects a serious absence of biblical authority among United Methodist leaders. Bishop Looney criticized the committee at this point, noting it had created a potentially divisive situation around an issue "clearly defined" as contrary to Christian principles. But while the committee did reach consensus that all references to homosexuality in the Bible were negative, members disagreed on whether the references applied for today. [An easy way to dismiss the clear biblical witness on the matter.] The four who voted against the recommendation (Richard Looney, David Seamands, James Holsinger, and William Lux) believe the biblical references are valid today.

Evangelicals are not distressed about this because they are homophobic. They are distressed by the likelihood that if church leaders can't find an authoritative word from Scripture about homosexual practice, they probably can't find an authoritative word about anything. This action underscores the great need for United Methodism to reclaim a commitment to vital biblical authority.

Another disquieting thought about this recommendation is that no less than five committee members who voted for it (Phil Wogaman, Arthur Pressley, Tex Sample, Victor Furnish, and Sally Geis) are noted faculty members at five of our official United Methodist seminaries (Wesley, Drew, St. Paul's, Perkins, and Iliff). It leaves many of us wondering whether, in this battle for spiritual and theological renewal, our seminary communities are friend or foe, problem or solution.

The battle about authority is not uncommon today. The Episcopal Church is struggling with its own sexuality debate with its maverick bishop John Spong. In his latest book, *Rescuing the Bible from Fundamentalism,* Spong claims the Virgin Birth is unthinkable, Jesus was not savior, and Paul was a repressed and "self-loathing" homosexual. Fellow Bishop William Frey, when asked whether the Episcopal Church will take any stand against such heresy, said, "The House of Bishops has shown itself to be impotent in the face of challenges to the core beliefs of the church. We've been paralyzed by our politeness." It all sounds so familiar.

But let those discouraged about the task force's action take heart. The report must be presented to the Executive Committee of the General Council on Ministries (GCOM) in September and to the full GCOM in December. When the task force makes its final report to the full GCOM, which is its parent body, GCOM has the authority to receive, modify, or otherwise perfect the report. GCOM could nullify the committee's request to change the statement. United Methodists should urge GCOM members to reject this divisive, controversial recommendation.

March/April 1991

Reflections on the
Homosexuality Study

· ·

*"The committee did provide a service for
the church. It clarified for us all, beyond
any question, just where the disagreements
are in United Methodism's debate about
human sexuality."*

THE report of the Committee to Study Homosexuality has been received by the General Council on Ministries (GCOM) and sent on to the 1992 General Conference. With the committee's work just concluded, let's reflect on it a bit.

First, the committee did provide a service for the church. It clarified for us all, beyond any question, just where the disagreements are in United Methodism's debate about human sexuality.

The committee's majority vs. minority impasse was illustrated perfectly during the committee's four-hour presentation to the GCOM in Chicago. On the one hand, Victor Furnish asked, "Can a covenantal, faithful, loving, committed gay or lesbian relationship ever be an expression of God's grace?" The majority group of the committee, I believe it is fair to say, would affirm such relationships can, indeed, be expressions of God's grace.

On the other hand, David Seamands spoke for the minority of four members of the committee (but for the majority of United Methodists) when he affirmed, "There is no ethical complexity regarding sexual norms in Scripture. The biblical norm is heterosexual, monogamous marriage. Anything else is outside the will of God."

Those are the two opposing views. They are mutually exclusive. Both can't be true for the church.

Second, Bishop Richard Looney (South Georgia) was right when he stated in his presentation that keeping the church's present standards keeps the United Methodist Church faithful to its constituency. It also keeps us faithful to mainstream Christian thought world-wide.

Phil Wogaman, a principal drafter of the committee's report, charged that it would be harmful to retain the present language condemning homosexual behavior as sin. Better, he said, to back away and say we aren't sure while we continue to study. He added that the burden of proof should be borne by those embracing language of condemnation (such as is presently in the *Book of Discipline*).

This is an amazing claim! The truth is, our present United Methodist standards keep us right in the mainstream of Christian thought and tradition on human sexuality. The church has been consistent in its teaching and understanding of homosexuality across the centuries. Our present standards are consistent with the Roman Catholic and Eastern Orthodox Churches, with theologians the likes of Karl Barth, Helmut Thielicke, and Albert Outler, as well as with studies done recently by the Disciples of Christ, the Presbyterians, the United Church of Christ, Episcopalians as well as the standards of the member churches of the National Association of Evangelicals (NAE). In addition, our own United Methodist Social Principles statement has served us well since 1972 and has been reaffirmed more convincingly with every General Conference vote since.

The fact is, the burden of proof rests squarely and heavily upon those who would change the church's moral teaching after so many years. What definitive, latter day teaching has come along to justify changing the church's sure moral standard?

A third thought. The church talks a lot about justice these days. As I watched the committee at its final meetings at Lake Junaluska and then in Chicago, with only four panel members representing the church's present position (and the biblical position) on homosexual practice, my spirit kept saying, "This is so unfair. It simply is not right. The representation is unjust."

I don't blame the committee members for the imbalance. They didn't select their own committee. The GCOM did that. But I do wonder why during the past three years that someone representing the majority of the committee (or GCOM for that matter) didn't stand up in quiet protest and say, "Friends, we have a terribly unjust situation in the makeup of this committee. As a matter of fairness, we need to ask GCOM to find a way to correct it to get better balance."

What if the committee's imbalance had been reversed, with only five or six persons representing the church's liberal wing. Would the process have been acceptable? Considered fair or credible? I think we know the answer. Most likely we would have seen Affirmation, the Methodist Federation for Social Action and other interest groups demonstrating publicly at the panel's meetings. Why was this injustice not acknowledged?

Finally, David Seamands reminded the GCOM in his presentation that we are a global church. That "what we do here" sends a message to world Methodism. David said, "I was ordained by an Indian bishop in Hyderabad. I know the stance of the church in India" (and he included Japan, Korea, Africa, etc.). He concluded with a plea from the Third World that should haunt us. It comes from the Rev. Dr. Sundo Kim, pastor of the 50,000-member Kwang Lim Methodist Church in Seoul, who said to David during a recent visit to America, "When you ask us to approve of this (homosexual behavior), you are asking us to consider as moral behavior that which is considered immoral by our non-Christian neighbors."

The Third-World church may be leading the First-World church sooner than we had thought.

January/February 1992

To Reconcile or Transform?

. . . .

*"The two programs—Reconciling and
Transforming—offer two very different
concepts of ministry to homosexual
persons."*

MINNEAPOLIS's large Hennepin Avenue United Methodist Church recently declared itself a "Reconciling Congregation." What is a Reconciling Congregation?

The Reconciling Congregation Program (RCP) was launched in 1984 by the unofficial caucus, Affirmation—United Methodists for Lesbian, Gay and Bisexual Concerns. Its purpose is to affirm the participation of homosexuals and lesbians in the life of the church.

While the RCP sounds compassionate, discerning United Methodists realize that implicit in the program is the dogma that, (1) homosexuality is a good gift of God and, (2) homosexual practice should be affirmed and celebrated in the church.

In *Open Hands* (Fall 1988), Affirmation's journal for the RCP, Ann Thompson Cook wrote, "We can and must give explicitly positive messages about homosexuality." In a promotional booklet distributed by the RCP, Cook disputes the possibility of healing for homosexuals, saying homosexuality cannot be cured any more than heterosexuality can be cured.

As a more hopeful and helpful option, the Evangelical Renewal Fellowship of the California-Nevada Annual Conference gave birth to the Transforming Congregations Program (TCP) in 1988. Its purpose: to affirm the biblical witness that homosexual practice is sin, and that the power of the Holy Spirit is available to transform the life of the homosexual. Its focus is on healing and integration of all repentant persons into local church membership.

The two programs—Reconciling and Transforming—offer two very different concepts of ministry to homosexuals. The RCP is one of tolerance and acceptance of all persons, especially homosexuals. It views homosexuality as something to be affirmed—not changed or healed. The TCP, however, accepts the biblical teaching (and United Methodist Church view) that homosexual behavior is "incompatible with Christian teaching," and believes God's grace can heal.

The troubling reality for United Methodists is that while the 1992 General Conference affirmed biblical standards, many of our bishops, boards of ordained ministry, and district superintendents embrace the views of the RCP. In fact, four annual conferences have voted to become "Reconciling Annual Conferences" which creates a crisis of conscience for many United Methodist clergy.

The truth is, the pro-gay RCP, while talking much about reconciliation, is one of the most divisive programs in the United Methodist Church today. The decimation of the Williamston (Michigan) UM Church is a tragic case in point. The sad tale is told by a Williamston layman and newspaper publisher, John McGoff, in the current *Transforming Congregations* (April–June 1993) newsletter. The Williamston pastor, the Rev. Ilona Sabo-Shuler, participated in the gay covenant service at the Broadway United Methodist Church in Indianapolis last July (1992). Following that service, Sabo-Shuler declined an offer to become a district superintendent and returned to Williamston. But she kept urging her church to join the RCP. Opposition toward the Rev. Sabo-Shuler's efforts grew, and by late fall some 97 members unsuccessfully requested her removal as pastor. Aggressive RCP lobbying continued. When the vote was finally taken, the RCP lost by 97 to 74.

The crusade, however, had been a calamity for the Williamston church. Despite profound alienation in the congregation, Michigan Bishop Donald Ott stood behind the Rev. Sabo-Shuler. Then, at the Williamston church's January Charge Conference, an extraordinarily non-reconciling thing took place.

The Nominating Committee report said, shockingly, "After prayerful consideration of all nominations, it does not look like you [those who were among the opposition to the RCP] are ready to work toward healing. Therefore, the Nominating Committee has decided to withdraw your name as we feel this is a bad time to put forth your nomination." Angered and hurt, some 30–40 members walked out of the charge conference. Some 80–100 members, including McGoff, received letters saying that they had been removed from leadership positions. Sunday morning worship attendance at Williamston, which usually numbered about 200, hit a low of 50 on a recent Sunday this spring. All of this, mind you, was over becoming a "Reconciling Congregation."

I am uneasy with all the talk these days about "reconciliation" and "ministry." The RCP is about neither. It is about power and imposed social change on UMs by those whose legislative attempts have failed at the last five General Conferences. The sooner the rest of us understand that, the better prepared we will be to deal with it.

July/August 1993

Will the United Methodist Church Enforce Its Standards?

"The United Methodist Church now has to decide whether it has the will to enforce its standards on sexuality. To do so will be a compassionate, not an unloving, act."

THE warm days of July brought two differing testimonies. One was from the Rev. Jeanne Audrey Powers, associate general secretary [now retired] of the General Commission on Christian Unity and Interreligious Concerns (GCCUIC), who publicly identified herself as a lesbian in her address at the Reconciling Congregations Convocation in Minneapolis on July 15.

The second was the testimony of a quiet United Methodist layman from Nevada, Ron Dennis, a leader in the Transforming Congregations Program. Ron shared his witness in a seminar at Good News' Summer Celebration in Cincinnati the same day Ms. Powers spoke in Minneapolis.

The two testimonies reflect the substantive differences that exist within United Methodism concerning homosexuality and lesbianism. Between 75–80 percent of United Methodist delegates since 1972 have voted to retain in our *Discipline* the biblically-based phrase that the practice of homosexuality is "incompatible with Christian teaching"; 20–25 percent want it deleted.

Ms. Powers said in her address "I have been a lesbian all my life. I've never known my identity as otherwise." Mr. Dennis recalls a family in which his father was not around much and where little affection was expressed. Ms. Powers views her lesbianism as a "gift of God." Mr. Dennis said, "Most people in the gay lifestyle know they are wrong."

Ms. Powers tells of finding acceptance among leaders of the United Methodist Church, even among some bishops who she knew were aware of her lesbianism. Mr. Dennis attended a Metropolitan Community Church (MCC) pastored by MCC founder, the Rev. Troy Perry, where he (surprisingly!) accepted Christ as Savior, yet didn't view his homosexuality as sin. In the months following, while reading the Scriptures, Mr. Dennis realized that the practice was wrong and the Lord delivered him from it.

Ms. Powers was quoted in the *Minneapolis Star Tribune* (7/14/95) saying, "God was leading me to make this public."

Mr. Dennis told his seminar, "Kids are being told today that gay is okay. But that's the snare of the devil."

Ms. Powers said, "I was partnered for 17 years and divorce was as painful to me as it might be to anyone in this room." Mr. Dennis said, "The Lord changed me and I had seven wonderful years with a beautiful wife, until her death."

Ms. Powers' "courageous" announcement will shock many United Methodists. Some have said it will be a catalyst for "dialogue." But Ms. Powers has said this is "a political act of resistance to false teachings that have contributed to heresy and homophobia in the Church."

Those of us among the 75–80 percent who affirm the biblical (and the United Methodist) position on homosexuality are called *heretics, homophobes,* and of course, *heterosexists.* These terms, obviously, are not terms of dialogue, but of condemnation and denunciation.

The *Star Tribune* quotes Ms. Powers as saying, "It seemed to me the time was ripe to use my experience, reputation, well-known name and credibility [and national United Methodist office] to help advance that cause." One obvious question is how the church can continue to pay Ms. Powers' salary in light of Par. 906.12 of the *Discipline,* which prohibits use of United Methodist funds (staff salaries) "to promote the acceptance of homosexuality."

More disturbing than all this is the fact that our American society is awash in confusion about sexual moral practices. (*Newsweek* recently ran a cover story on "Bisexuality.") The Christian Church remains the only institution that can provide reliable guidelines for our society about what God intended for man and woman.

The United Methodist Church now has to decide whether it has the will to enforce its standards on sexuality. To do so will be a compassionate, not an unloving, act. Dr. Armand M. Nicholi II, longtime director of Student Health Services at Harvard, once spoke of the danger of normalizing homosexuality. "Many in our society today deny the pathology of homosexuality, refuse to consider its moral implications, and tend to view it as a form of sexual expression that merely 'differs' from the statistical norm. Such attitudes, though appearing humane and altruistic, act to destroy the well-being of the homosexual. They not only discourage his seeking available help, but also encourage him to resign himself to a life which clinical evidence reveals to be increasingly lonely and frustrating, regardless of how permissive and accepting our society becomes . . . . Clinical experience has demonstrated that motivation to change plus conscious feelings of guilt significantly increase the prospect of therapeutic success."

With Ron Dennis, we believe that there is power to overcome sin through the Holy Spirit. This should be the message our church proclaims.

September/October 1995

Who's Following COCU?

"United Methodists need to be aware that the Episcopal Church has put COCU on the shelf for now and won't even reconsider it until the year 2000 . . . . Episcopal leaders didn't believe the plan takes theology seriously."

ONE of the most important issues coming to our 1996 General Conference is the proposal from the Consultation on Church Union (COCU). The plan, found in the document *Churches in Covenant Communion: The Church of Christ Uniting,* would unite nine Protestant denominations. The new entity would be called the Church of Christ Uniting.

The consultation has been discussing church union for 35 years, but in recent years, two things have become clear. One, all of the participating communions would affirm and seek the unity of God's church. Two, they have always refused anything that looks like a merger of their denominations.

The proposal now on the table will bring the nine denominations into "covenant communion." It is carefully worded to state that it is not organic union or merger. I believe the COCU leaders are convinced it is not merger. To others, however, the open-ended and undefined "covenant communion" step, which will be realized in the year 2000, still looks and sounds like a prelude to, if not an actual, merger. It will simply happen a step at a time. The plan states: "In covenant communion the churches may maintain, *for so long as each may determine, their own church structures and traditions*" (p. 9, emphasis mine). What slips through almost accidentally in that statement is the intent to eventually unite "structures and traditions." COCU began years ago as a movement to merge. One wonders if the only real change in the new plan is terminology, for the sake of getting some proposal passed.

Nonetheless, United Methodism appears to be on a course to approve the plan. The United Methodist Council of Bishops took action at its spring meeting to recommend to General Conference that it "adopt the covenanting proposal" and "approve the text *Churches in Covenant Communion* as the basis for agreement to join with other participating churches." The bishops also recommended five changes in the *Book of Discipline* that would be needed, one being a change in Article 5 of our United Methodist Constitution.

United Methodists need to be aware that the Episcopal Church has put COCU on the shelf for now and won't even reconsider it until the year 2000. That church's committee report said, "By attempting to be all things to all church traditions, COCU has proposed a way to reconcile diverse forms of ministry which, upon close examination, asks for a sign without substance and a union without real reconciliation." Episcopal leaders didn't believe the plan takes theology seriously.

The General Assembly of the Presbyterian Church (USA) took action this summer to refer the plan back to committee with a number of "expressed concerns." Those concerns are substantive for Presbyterians, dealing with what would be constitutional changes in their *Book of Order*. The assembly also heard concerns that the two COCU documents may not be compatible with Reformed theology and polity and so took action referring them to its Office of Theology and Worship for careful study.

COCU chief Daniel C. Hamby was reported in *Newscope* as claiming there were "wrinkles" that the Presbyterians had to iron out, but that they were definitely coming into the covenant communion. However, some Presbyterian leaders say this is not so. They claim the issues are substantive and that the Presbyterians have agreed to enter into discussion of the plan but will not decide to come in until the covenant agreement becomes acceptable and problematic issues are resolved.

Few United Methodists seem to know much at all about the proposal. Some pastors are unaware of it's being considered. Others know few of the plan's specifics. For example, most haven't considered what "mutual recognition of ordained ministries" really means; or that once the "covenant communion" is inaugurated, "there will be no more ordinations carried out in denominational isolation from the other covenanting churches" (p. 24). Do we realize what this means in light of a COCU newsletter's report that the United Church of Christ approved the plan this summer but had appended to its acceptance the caveat that the ordination of gay, lesbian, and bi-sexual persons was a "gift" which the UCC brings to COCU? That "gift" of course, is prohibited for us by our United Methodist *Book of Discipline*. The UCC also noted it would not be compelled to baptize in the name of the Father, Son, and Holy Spirit. What kind of unity can there be when scriptural standards are so easily set aside?

Geoffrey Wainwright, professor at the Duke Divinity School and longtime ecumenist, gave this word of caution about COCU recently: "True ecumenism aims at unity in the true Christian faith. We mustn't go into an institutional unity in which the faith of biblical and classic Christianity is compromised."

United Methodists should get the COCU documents, study and discuss them, and let their delegations know their views. We dare not end up approving an open-ended and little understood plan of "covenant communion" in Denver simply because we failed to study the proposal carefully.

Note: *The 1996 General Conference approved United Methodism's participation in COCU. The uniting service is set for the Advent season of the year 2000.*

November/December 1995

Moving Ahead, Attuned to the Times, But Doctrinally Adrift

· ·

"The chasm between United Methodist leadership and orthodox, Bible-believing laity seems wider and more pronounced than ever."

As THE eleven days of General Conference in Denver fade, all of us are trying to discern what happened there and what it meant. Clearly, it's a mixed bag, but it does provide a portrait of what's happening within United Methodism. We plunge boldly ahead, long on style, short on substance; attuned to the times, light years from the Apostolic faith; ambassadors of inclusivity, practitioners of institutional and theological exclusivity. Everything is acceptable except orthodoxy. I want to reflect further about the significance of several of those actions.

HOMOSEXUALITY

The homosexual issue dominated this General Conference like never before. From Bishop Judith Craig's opening episcopal address until the final evening session, this issue was continually thrust before the delegates. It nearly held them hostage.

The caucuses pushing the church to change its standards on sexuality conducted a well-orchestrated, in-your-face campaign with team members opening the doors at the convention center, holding public rallies, distributing newsletters and handouts, and even placing welcome mats outside the delegates' hotel rooms.

Despite support from the episcopal address and from 15 dissident bishops who released a public statement expressing their "pain" at the church's present standards on homosexuality, the delegates continued to say a firm "no" to the campaign for change. They voted, once again, to retain the church's Scriptural position by approximately a 70–75 percent vote.

It's important for United Methodists to know that the liberal recommendation out of committee to replace the familiar statement in the Social Principles that homosexuality is "incompatible with Christian teaching" with the statement "we are unable to arrive at a common mind" verbiage was defeated by a 60.4 percent vote.

Four years ago, *an identical recommendation out of committee was defeated by a 61.5 percent vote*. The difference between the 1992 and 1996 votes is negligible. Note that the votes above were to defeat a liberal majority report. Four years ago, when the majority report was defeated, and the minority report (presented by David Seamands) became the majority, it was approved by a 74 percent vote. This time, the chair ruled (we believe correctly) that the minority report (presented again by David Seamands) needed no vote because it simply asked to "retain" the present language in the *Discipline*.

Here's the point: Had the chair gone ahead to call for a vote on the Seamands minority report, which had become the majority report, it undoubtedly would have prevailed by about a 74 percent vote once again. The vote to retain the prohibition against funding gay caucuses (Par. 906.12) was retained by exactly a 74 percent majority.

So, despite the full-court press in Denver, the delegates resisted the effort to alter the church standards on homosexuality by nearly the *identical margin* that they did in 1992.

THE 15 DISSENTING BISHOPS

Just three days into the conference, 15 United Methodist bishops released to the secular press their statement confessing their "pain" about the church's present standards on homosexuality. The action sent shock waves throughout the conference, the city of Denver, and across the church. It hit the Internet and the Denver papers before the other bishops even knew about it. A number of bishops were furious about the release and felt betrayed by their colleagues. The release of the statement by the "Denver 15" was considered by many a serious breach of episcopal protocol, as bishops traditionally are not supposed to influence the legislative process at General Conference. More seriously, it was also a breach of trust as these episcopal leaders, charged with upholding the doctrine and order of the church, came out in *opposition* to their church's standards on homosexuality—and in opposition to biblical norms.

The full Council of Bishops, having been called upon for some kind of response to what the dissident bishops had done, met behind closed doors for several days to discuss and prepare a response. Reports are that it was as stormy and painful a time as many older bishops could remember. After five days, the Council released a statement simply reaffirming the church's present standards and their commitment to "teach and uphold those standards." Some of the bishops wanted a stronger statement than the one issued. At least three bishops have already released statements to their delegations expressing more firmly their disagreement with the action of the "Denver 15."

This whole episode may be the catalyst for the Council of Bishops to face up to and admit that they have serious, deeply felt differences as a Council. This would be far healthier than their long-standing pattern of projecting an appearance of unity that is not there. Such an admission would be welcomed by the church and would assure members that their episcopal leaders are not walking in an uncritical lockstep.

Many questions remain about this unprecedented action. One is, how can the 15 bishops "in good conscience" agree to the statement from the Council that assures us all that the bishops, collectively and individually, will "teach and uphold our church's doctrine and discipline"? How can they in good faith "teach" what they have just publicly repudiated?

We pray for courage and candor from the other bishops who disagree with the dissident 15. Theologian Stephen Hutchens wrote recently some words relevant to this whole matter: "What shall Christ say to those who are not even willing to sacrifice collegial relations for the sake of truth? How shall they look into the eyes of the martyrs?" Truth must never get lost amidst collegiality.

THE BAPTISM STUDY

What about the Baptism study? According to our Good News board member, Riley Case, the committee has been sensitive to evangelical feedback and has responded accordingly with revisions. The result is an improved document that evangelicals can live with. He believes the study moved from baptismal regeneration to an emphasis that salvation requires saving faith; it moved from a view that infant baptism was complete in itself to an acknowledgment that infant baptism must lead to public profession.

COCU

Delegates voted to approve participation in Churches of Christ Uniting (COCU), though we suspect many haven't a clue about what exactly they approved. An amendment guaranteeing that United Methodist standards for ordained ministry will stand firm for clergy transferring into the United Methodist Church helped alleviate fears of some delegates about gay and lesbian ordinations currently taking place in the United Church of Christ (UCC). While we have not been enthusiastic about COCU, the uniting service will not take place until Advent of the year 2000 and United Methodist ecumenical leader, Dr. Bruce Robbins, assures us that local church participation in COCU is totally voluntary.

MOOD OF THE CONFERENCE

Seasoned General Conference watchers sensed a different mood at the Denver conference. That may reflect more intercessory prayer being offered than we can remember. One factor in this change of mood was in the election of legislative committee officers. This time, officers included many moderates and several clearly identified evangelicals. The same was true for sub-committee chairs. This reflects a trend of emerging moderate voices moving into leadership positions at General Conference, and that helped make for less volatile and more measured debate. That trend will continue.

In addition, the evangelical network at Denver was as broad and as strong as it has ever been. As we have said elsewhere, this network is alive, well, growing, and finding ways to work cooperatively like never before. This, too, will continue.

Finally, the Central Conference delegates are becoming a definite force on the floor of the conference. This happened some in Louisville, but much more this time in Denver. Most all of these delegates are thoroughly orthodox in their moral and theological convictions.

MORAL AND THEOLOGICAL DEBATE

As we look at major addresses and floor debate, we fall short at several points. First, United Methodism must recover an integrity of language in the church. George Orwell, in his essay, "Politics and the English Language," noted that "Those who would change a culture corrupt its language, particularly by hiding the reality of an evil they desire behind a less revealing name."

For eleven days we heard pro-gay advocates and other church leaders speak about "welcoming" gays and lesbians into the church. But what was really being advocated was not just hospitality but *an approval of gay and lesbian practice*. This was never stated explicitly, however. What that leaves is a good and wholesome term (*hospitality*) being used but which has been injected with new meaning: homosexual practice is acceptable. The result: those who oppose the church approving homosexual practice are seen as "inhospitable" and unloving.

The attitudes expressed toward evangelical and orthodox Christians in the episcopal address is another concern, especially if it reflects the thinking of the full Council toward those of an evangelical persuasion.

The stacking of pejorative phrases in subtle reference to those seeking doctrinal fidelity is not the language of dialogue but of dismissal.

Bishop Craig warned of "destructive controversy," of engagement which "scatters seeds of dissension and destruction," that we can be "dams of self-interest and polluted channels of selfish motives," of her fear that the "desire to protect" may turn to "desire to control," of our need to "repent of our pretentious assumptions," and the temptation that we "stand so rigidly in tradition." Let's be sure of one thing. Those pejorative descriptions are not referring to the liberal and progressive wing of the church. They reflect deep-seated impressions about evangelicalism that preempt any meaningful dialogue.

The chasm between United Methodist leadership and orthodox, Bible-believing laity seems wider and more pronounced than ever. When the Confessing Movement's call for restoring the Lordship of Christ is viewed by seminary professors and prominent pastors as something repugnant, we know we have serious, unresolved problems.

Someone has said that sound doctrine is not a corral that confines but a map that directs us to the goal of salvation. Or to change metaphors, it's a set of harbor buoys that show the navigable passages between God and humanity. Unfortunately, United Methodism seems still adrift doctrinally, unsure of the harbor buoys, and thus navigating by impulse and intuition. To sail safely, we must in the days ahead give prayerful and urgent attention to reforming our church by conforming it to the requirements of God's Word.

May/June 1996

A Matter of Trust

· ·

"Can we trust our episcopal leaders who have said they 'are committed, collectively and individually, to teach and uphold our church's doctrine and discipline'?"

LYLE Schaller, respected United Methodist author and church consultant, wrote in the UM pastors' journal, *Circuit Rider,* several years ago that "A serious erosion of trust exists between some denominational officials and many of the leaders of the largest congregations."

The issue of trust remains for United Methodists today, particularly in the area of the homosexuality debate. This was the context for the Good News board's challenge to the Council of Bishops in September to "adhere to, in practice as well as in teaching, the doctrinal standards and moral principles of the church."

Why such a challenge? Quite simply, because of what has continued to happen since General Conference.

In Denver, we recall, 15 of our bishops released a statement saying that while affirming their vows as bishops, they declared, "However, we must confess the pain we feel over our personal convictions that are contradicted by the proscriptions in the *Discipline* against gay and lesbian persons within our church and within our ordained and diaconal ministers."

Since the United Methodist proscription against ordination is for "self-avowed, practicing homosexuals," we conclude the pain felt is for those "practicing" who cannot be ordained as United Methodist clergy.

Following several tumultuous days and numerous meetings in Denver, the bishops released a statement saying they "are committed, collectively and individually, to teach and uphold our church's doctrine and discipline." The question of trust remains, however, as we examine what has happened since Denver.

First, at this spring's annual conference sessions, two more conferences voted to become "Reconciling Annual Conferences," those being the Wisconsin and Oregon–Idaho Annual Conferences. (The Troy, California/ Nevada, Northern Illinois, and New York Conferences have previously so voted.) The "Reconciling" movement is described as "a movement of churches and individuals who are working for the full inclusion of lesbian, gay, and bisexual people." Already, groups of evangelical/traditional pastors have had to meet in both of those annual conferences and produce "Declarations" saying they will not be bound by the action.

Second, the New England Annual Conference voted last spring to "study" whether or not to become a "Reconciling Annual Conference" at next year's session. Recently, several pastors in that conference have reported feeling pressured to attend district "study" meetings where materials being "studied" include a "Reconciling Congregation" video and materials. The church's official position is not strongly presented, they report.

Third, last spring the Oregon/ Idaho Annual Conference voted into full membership and ordained as elder Ms. Jeanne Knepper. Jeanne is a woman about whom her Board of Ordained Ministry (BOM) said several years ago, "We believe Jeanne Knepper is what the General Conference describes in the *Book of Discipline* as a 'self-avowed practicing homosexual.'" Jeanne was appointed this spring by Bishop William Dew to Shalom Ministries, a ministry of the Metropolitan District of the Oregon/Idaho Conference. In the August newsletter, "Shalom To You," Jeanne wrote that the General Conference action regarding covenant services is "unenforceable." In a following article she shared the meditation used at a recent "covenant" service she conducted for "Erin and Kim." In her July newsletter, she wrote poignantly how just two days after her ordination, Alice Knotts (Knepper's partner) told her that "she was leaving me to begin a new life in Denver." (Alice is also a clergy member of the Oregon/Idaho Conference.)

All this brings us back to the issue of "trust." Can we trust our episcopal leaders who have said they "are committed, collectively and individually, to teach and uphold our church's doctrine and discipline"? Right now, we're unsure.

For many United Methodists, this much-debated matter is not tangential but "strikes at the root." It has enormous implications. Eminent German theologian, Wolfhart Pannenberg, a world-renowned scholar, recently touched on those implications. Writing in the *Church Times* in Britain, he said: "Those who urge the church to change the norm of its teaching on this matter must know that they are promoting schism. If a church were to let itself be pushed to the point where it ceased to treat homosexual activity as a departure from the biblical norm, and recognized homosexual unions as a personal partnership of love equivalent to marriage, such a church would stand no longer on biblical ground but against the unequivocal witness of Scripture. A church that took this step would cease to be the one, holy, catholic, and apostolic church."

We wait, prayerfully and soberly, to see if our bishops are, indeed, "committed, collectively and individually, to teach and uphold our church's doctrine and discipline."

January/February 1997

Church-Busters Doing Irreparable Harm

"The debate over homosexuality is of critical importance for United Methodism because of its broader implications. It forces the church to identify its locus of authority. Is Scripture truly authoritative?"

IF United Methodism is serious about halting its plummeting membership and being faithful to biblical truth, it must come to grips with its "church-busters." These are the pastors and leaders who are doing irreparable harm to local United Methodist churches by pushing upon them the pro-homosexual agenda. They do so in direct violation of our denominational standards on homosexual practice.

Consider this recent and disturbing example. On September 14, Rev. Jimmy Creech, senior pastor of the 1,900-member First United Methodist Church in Omaha, Nebraska, conducted a service of union between two lesbian members in the church. He did so against the wishes of Nebraska Area Bishop Joel Martinez. In 1990, Rev. Creech was pastor of the 1,000-member Fairmont United Methodist Church in Raleigh, N.C. He was a "church-buster" there as well. His pro-homosexual crusade brought agonizing turmoil and membership loss to that church, which asked that he not be reappointed.

Creech came to First United Methodist Church, Omaha, in 1996, and already it is experiencing a similar upheaval. Several members have filed a grievance against him for conducting the service. We must pray for the bishop as our denomination tries to hold a pastor accountable.

The sad thing about this is that something quite destructive is happening to the Omaha church. One member, Helen Howell, who serves on both the Staff Parish Relations committee and the Ad Council, told the *Omaha World-Herald,* "I think what he is doing is awful. It goes against the Bible. It goes against the *Discipline.* And it will split the church." It has already begun to do so. Other United Methodist churches have had similar experiences, resulting in losses of both members and finances.

Several questions must be asked about this present crusade. First, do we have any idea of the damage being done to local church ministry by the growing public perception that the United Methodist Church is not clear about the wrongness and unhealthfulness of homosexual practice? Through the few articles that have already appeared in Omaha newspapers, the ministries of other United Methodist churches in Omaha have been affected.

Second, are United Methodists fully aware of what is being espoused by the pro-homosexual lobby in our church? At the "Reconciling Congregations" national conference in Atlanta last summer, retired United Methodist Bishop Dale White called resistance to the Reconciling (pro-homosexual) cause a "demonic phenomenon." Retired Bishop Melvin Wheatley said that "Gayness is good. In many ways it's better than straightness." Is homosexuality really good? Certainly, we affirm that God's grace is available to all. But is homosexual practice really good? The average American male will live to 76 years of age. Research has been done showing that the average male practicing homosexuality will live to age 41. If he has AIDS, he will live to age 39. Allowing for even a considerable margin of error, can a lifestyle this destructive be considered "good"?

Richard John Neuhaus, editor of *First Things,* believes the pro-homosexual movement peaked in 1993 and is losing momentum. He says that "after three decades of strenuous effort and high confidence of victory, the demand for the formal approval of homosexuality has been turned back again and again even in the liberal old-line Protestant churches. . . . Despite the overwhelming support of . . . the major culture-forming institutions of our society . . . the American people have not been induced to take the fateful step of affirming homosexuality as a good thing." That is true for United Methodists.

Finally, will the United Methodist Church really affirm the primacy of Scripture in its faith and practice? The debate over homosexuality is of critical importance for United Methodism because of its broader implications. It forces the church to identify its locus of authority. Is Scripture truly authoritative? Or will we give lip service to Scriptural authority while allowing virtual autonomy to our pastors and theologians to reconstruct and reinterpret biblical texts at will?

Ultimately, the church will have to choose between the authority of the Bible or the authority of human-centered standards—"my faith journey" or "my experience." John Stott, known world-wide as author, evangelist and theologian, reminds us in his new commentary on Romans that "the only context which he [God] intends for the 'one flesh' experience is heterosexual monogamy, and that a homosexual partnership (however loving and committed it may claim to be) is 'against nature' and can never be regarded as a legitimate alternative to marriage" (*Romans: God's Good News for the World,* InterVarsity, 1994).

While we affirm the sacred worth of all persons, the United Methodist Church must be clear that those practicing homosexuality are not helped, and many lives are even seriously damaged, by those who seek, however well intentioned, the church's blessing upon a practice proscribed by Scripture and by the United Methodist *Book of Discipline.*

November/December 1997

A Crisis That Demands Resolution—The Creech Verdict

"Where is the expressed indignation on behalf of life-long United Methodists who are being forced out of the only church home they have ever known? Where is the expressed indignation on behalf of 300 'exiled' members of First United Methodist Church in Omaha who are now meeting for worship in a school building?"

THE United Methodist Church is reeling amidst unprecedented waves of distress and turmoil. On Friday, March 13, two events occurred which have shaken our denomination. The first was the acquittal of the Rev. Jimmy Creech, the Omaha, Nebraska, pastor who faced a church trial for performing a lesbian marriage last September. A jury of 13 clergy voted 8–5 that he had indeed violated the "order and discipline of the church." Unfortunately, nine votes were needed to convict. So he was not found guilty.

The second event was the release of a statement that same afternoon (before the verdict was announced) publicly declaring the intent of 92 United Methodist clergy from across the country "to celebrate rites of union with all couples, regardless of gender." The group, calling itself "Proclaiming the Vision," pledged to "continue to perform [same-sex] covenant services as a part of our pastoral role. . . ." Concerning the 1996 General Conference action prohibiting same-sex unions, they flaunted, ". . . we will not be bound by it."

The number of clergy has since grown to 120 and will surely be more by the time you are reading this. Their "courageous public statement," as the group described it, constitutes an act of unprecedented rebellion against the authority of the United Methodist Church and the clear intent of the 1996 General Conference.

Adding fuel to the already-raging fire, two annual conference cabinets—California/Nevada and the Troy (NY) conferences—recently released statements indicating their support of pastors who perform same-sex covenants. The cabinet of the California/Nevada Annual Conference affirmed its support of United Methodist pastors who perform same-sex marriages between "loving, committed life partners." It also expressed appreciation for the ministry of the Rev. Jimmy Creech.

In an attempt to clarify the position of the California/Nevada Conference, Bishop Melvin G. Talbert said in a subsequent statement, "At no point have the cabinet and I discussed operating outside the *Book of Discipline*." He went on to say, "We encourage all our pastors to do their ministry in compliance with the *Book of Discipline*."

The clarification, however, is unconvincing.

The Rev. Thomas Kimball, United Methodist superintendent of California/Nevada's Golden Gate District, publicly reported that the cabinet, headed by Bishop Talbert, had been asked to clarify what it would do "if one of our pastors came to us, saying that they wanted to perform a holy [same-sex] union." Kimball said the cabinet was "unequivocal" in supporting "the right of our pastors to be pastors in the local settings."

Speaking at a press conference hosted by San Francisco's Metropolitan Community Church (a homosexual denomination), Kimball also said the cabinet "affirmed" Bethany United

Methodist Church's (San Francisco) decision to continue performing covenant ceremonies for homosexual, lesbian, bisexual, and transgendered persons. Also speaking at the press conference, the Rev. Karen Oliveto, Bethany's pastor, said her church had been performing same-sex covenants for decades.

Clearly, this is not doing ministry "in compliance with the Book of *Discipline.*" Bishop Talbert should know that.

Bishop Susan M. Morrison and the district superintendents of the Troy Annual Conference also released a statement prior to the trial verdict supporting Creech's decision "to respond to the pastoral needs of members of his congregation by performing a service of holy union."

This reckless disregard for the order and discipline of the United Methodist Church is shocking.

Many United Methodists will remember that Bishops Talbert and Morrison were among the 15 bishops who publicly expressed their "pain" about the church's stance on homosexuality during the 1996 General Conference. The full Council of Bishops immediately released a statement in an attempt to calm troubled delegates and a confused church. It said, in part, "The Council understands the present language in *The Book of Discipline* to be a faithful expression of faith and discipleship and *are committed, collectively and individually, to teach and uphold our church's doctrine and discipline*" (emphasis added). It went on to say, "As General Superintendents and servants of the whole church, we affirm and respect the legislative authority of the General Conference."

Unfortunately, the actions of these two bishops noted above are not consistent with the public commitment made by the Council in Denver (cited above).

Three days after the Creech verdict and the statement by the 92 clergy, the leadership of Good News asked the United Methodist Council of Bishops to call a special session of General Conference as soon as possible to address the crisis. Others did the same, including the Confessing Movement, Dr. Maxie Dunnam, Dr. Bill Hinson, and Bishop Marion Edwards and the twelve district superintendents of the North Carolina Annual Conference.

It will take a special session of General Conference to resolve this crisis decisively. Delegates to the 1996 General Conference in Denver voted to add a sentence to a statement on marriage in Par. 65C of *The Book of Discipline*, which said, "Ceremonies that celebrate homosexual unions shall not be conducted by our ministers and shall not be conducted in our churches." It was passed by a resounding 74 percent vote. The placement of this sentence in the "Social Principles" portion of *The Book of Discipline*, however, has resulted in questions for some about the binding authority of the prohibitive statement.

This is one of the issues that must be addressed at a special session of General Conference. The above sentence should be moved to a section in the *Discipline*, perhaps on "Ordained Ministry," where it would be clearly juridical, that is, legally binding. A special session must also send a clear directive to our bishops that same-sex unions—homosexual marriages—will not be allowed, and that disciplinary actions will be taken against those pastors who ignore the church's policy on such unions.

Our bishops need to be admonished, as never before, about their responsibility "for carrying into effect the rules, regulations, and responsibilities prescribed and enjoined by the General Conference . . ." (Par. 45, Article III, *Discipline*).

Some are saying already that a special session of General Conference would be too expensive. Quite simply, it will be too expensive not to have such a session. Also, with minimum creativity, the church can find ways to reduce greatly the costs of a two-day, one-night special session of General Conference. Costs could be cut by holding it in one of our tall steeple churches in Dallas, Houston, or Atlanta; by encouraging local churches to help underwrite travel costs of delegates; by forfeiting the use of hi-tech electronic voting for this abbreviated session; and by drawing on the enormous net assets presently being held by our major program boards. Finances should not prevent the church from doing whatever is necessary to arrive at a clear and convincing resolution of this matter.

If such resolution does not take place, many United Methodists have indicated they will have no other recourse than to find ways to express their own conscience through redirection of money that will be disruptive to church programs at every level.

Finally, we expect more from our bishops than mere recitation of church policy. While it is true that church policy remains the same, churches are currently being devastated and divided by the crusade of a relatively small number of United Methodists who continue to push a radically revisionist moral standard that the church's General Conference has rejected since 1972.

Where is the expressed indignation on behalf of life-long United Methodists who are being forced out of the only church home they have ever known? Where is the expressed indignation on behalf of 300 "exiled" members of First United Methodist Church in Omaha who are now meeting for worship in a school building? Where is the expressed indignation at more than 120 United Methodist pastors who have declared publicly their intent to "celebrate rites of union with all couples, regardless of gender"? Dr. David Seamands properly refers to this as "blessing the unblessable."

Why is the episcopal indignation more likely to be saved for those churches who admit prayerfully that they are struggling with their stewardship responsibilities in light of United Methodism's moral and theological crises?

These 120 pastors and others who are like-minded should seek another church fellowship whose views are compatible with their own. This would be far more loving and healing for the church than their continued crusade to impose an unbiblical agenda that contradicts Scripture and 2000 years of Christian teaching.

The result of this current upheaval is that United Methodism faces a crisis today unlike anything I have seen since entering the ministry in 1967. Our members are troubled, de-moralized, deeply grieved, angry, confused, heart-sick, and wrestling with what they might do. At the same time, they are looking to the Council of Bishops with the hope that they will do more than just cite relevant portions of the *Discipline* and hope things will quiet down. United Methodists are praying and looking for leadership, trusting their bishops will "teach and uphold our church's doctrine and discipline" as they assured delegates in Denver they would do.

The church needs Holy Spirit-led leadership from the Council of Bishops. If the council does not respond with due diligence, United Methodism will continue to be toshsed to and fro by the waves of ecclesiastical disorder and moral anarchy.

May/June 1998

Five

Radical Feminism—The Unchallenged Controversy

Fairest Sophia

. . . .

*"We must find a way to mainstream the
goddess into the universe within which
women are actually living their lives."* —
Wisdom's Feast, p. 10.

"Fairest Sophia, Ruler of all nature,
O Thou in whom earth and heav'n are one,
Thee will I cherish, Thee will I honor,
Thou, my soul's glory, joy, and crown."

THE above hymn is from page 185 of *Wisdom's Feast*. A
eucharist to Sophia begins on page 162.

ONE is tempted simply to ignore this book about Sophia
as trendy nonsense. But two of the three authors of *Wisdom's
Feast* are United Methodist clergy. They are serious about this
business of worshiping "Sophia."

The controversy spawned in the Eastern Pennsylvania
Conference by United Methodist clergy teaching about a goddess named Sophia conveys the deplorable state of theological
discourse within United Methodism today. The issue, of course,
is not whether pastors Cady and Taussig are nice persons. The
issue is whether there are any limits to what United Methodists teach and preach. And, if our clergy exceed those limits,
what action must be taken and by whom? These critical questions must be dealt with.

Now, about the Sophia controversy, a few comments.

First, authors Cady and Taussig want to defuse the controversy by saying their book is merely "theological exploration" and "scholarly inquiry." This has become a popular appeal

in mainline churches today to justify nearly any new theological trend. And it usually works. It did so with the Eastern Pennsylvania Board of Ordained Ministry.

The only problem is, this claim simply is not true. United Methodists were being instructed about Sophia in Rev. Cady's home. In fact, *Wisdom's Feast* includes practical steps for bringing Sophia theology into church practice. For example, the book contains prayers, liturgies, litanies, and a eucharist to be used in worship experiences.

Actually, the book itself indicates this teaching is more than just scholarly inquiry and reflection by its authors. They say on p. 10, "We must find a way to mainstream the goddess into the universe within which women are actually living their lives." Don't miss that. They want to mainstream Sophia among United Methodist women. That's propagation, not just "scholarly inquiry" or "theological exploration."

Second, one must wonder what motivates this new teaching. Cady admits that during a communion service one day, she suddenly asked herself, "What am I doing? Celebrating the experience of some man? What does he have to do with me?" One wants to say warmly and pastorally, "Oh, He has everything to do with you. He died for you and for us all."

But beyond any pastoral comment, this is a day when Boards of Ordained Ministry are concerned about healthful attitudes among clergy. Cady's question from her earlier communion experience, "What am I doing? Celebrating the experience of some man?" reflects unhealthy, if not seriously affected, attitudes toward the male gender. Those are problems Boards of Ordained Ministry have to deal with pastorally, and that seems a far more sensible option than allowing a totally new theological system. Those of us ordained to United Methodist ministry have promised to preach, teach and tell the "old, old story" of "the experience of some man." That man, of course, is Jesus of Nazareth who died for us and rose again.

Third, one wonders why no United Methodist leaders were concerned that Jesus was being literally replaced by Sophia. Eric

Umile, a United Methodist layperson who encountered teachings about Sophia in his Eastern Pennsylvania Conference, was right on target with his charge, "It's not Christianity. It ignores Jesus Christ. These people are making a goddess the focus of their religious worship." What else can one conclude when Sophia is portrayed as walking on the water toward *her* disciples? To suggest that United Methodists sing the words "Fairest, Sophia, Ruler of all nature," most certainly will bring revulsion and disgust to most United Methodists and increase the exodus from our church.

Surely it's time for righteous anger. What is happening to the United Methodist witness? Are we not becoming a laughing-stock, an object of ridicule across the Christian world? *Wisdom's Feast* co-author Taussig says he thinks "most of the New Testament is not historical account." But in that statement, is he not already well outside the boundaries set for ordained United Methodist clergy?

One rightly asks, "Where is all this taking us?" Women's Week Celebration at Perkins School of Theology recently included a seminar by one who practices Dianic witchcraft. Where, indeed, are we going? Perkins professor, Billy Abraham, is right in saying we have had a free-for-all over the last generation and that "the church has no boundaries." At least we have none we are presently enforcing.

The United Methodist Church is at a crossroads today— as this kind of controversy illustrates perfectly. We need a whole new theological climate in the church. Nonsense such as Sophia theology simply must not be allowed. The church must find some mechanism to deal with this kind of unacceptable distortion of its message. Such a response would not reflect bigotry or intolerance, but rather a passion to be faithful to "the faith that was once for all entrusted to the saints" (Jude 3). It would recognize the fact that those entering the United Methodist ministry have made a personal and public covenant to be faithful to the Christian Gospel.

The church can't wait. It must attend to its theological crisis. The Gospel is being trivialized right before our eyes. If we don't face up to it now, thousands of United Methodist laity will protest the only way they know how—with their dollars and their letters of transfer.

July/August 1990

Phasing Out "Father"

....

"This trend in United Methodist God-language does not reflect 'diversity,' it reflects doctrinal disarray. One feels like grabbing the nearest phone and saying, 'Quick, operator, get me a biblical theologian!'"

Is United Methodism phasing out its use of the term "Father" in its public worship?

A few weeks ago I spent several hours studying the proposed new *Book of Worship,* a companion to our hymnal, used mainly by pastors in planning worship. (It still has to be approved by next year's General Conference.)

I surveyed its several hundred prayers to see the language used in addressing God. I wondered how many addressed God as "Father." What I found was disturbing.

I counted some 281 prayers in the book of worship resources, give or take a dozen. *Of that number, in only ten was God referred to as "Father."* That's right! Only ten times in some 281 prayers!

Of those prayers addressing God as "Father," one was a prayer of Charles Wesley, another was in John Wesley's Watchnight Service, another from a Syrian Orthodox prayer, etc. Prayers from another era. Four were carried over from the 1965 *Book of Worship*. And one was "O God our Mother and Father."

My conclusion: United Methodism is in the process of phasing out use of the term "Father" in our corporate worship and praying.

Equally disturbing is the presence of questionable terms that supposedly reflect our "diversity," such as: "O Mother God," "Bakerwoman God," "O God, our grove," "Grandfather, Great Spirit." And "God of wind, word, and fire."

This trend in United Methodist God-language does not reflect "diversity," it reflects doctrinal disarray. One feels like grabbing the nearest phone and saying, "Operator, quick, get me a biblical theologian!"

In the current *Circuit Rider,* our United Methodist pastors' journal, Jerome King Del Pino raises relevant questions about prayers to "Mother God," asking, "Should our church officially adopt such language? In doing so, have we abandoned biblical Christianity?" His questions are on target. The only problem is, *we're already doing it!* Our United Methodist seminaries mandate new God-language without any official church authorization for doing so. Ask our seminarians today whether they feel free to address God as "Father" at United Methodist seminaries. Many will say, "No, it isn't even up for debate. It could lower your grade."

The United Methodist church has given no mandate for imposing new God-language upon anyone. Let's remember that the 1984 General Conference *only received* [it did not adopt or approve] the inclusive language committee report, *Words That Hurt and Words That Heal.* It intentionally did not approve or adopt it. And the Judicial Council ruled that *it is not* a binding document for United Methodists.

Still, the new language is being imposed upon seminarians and laity, even though it may violate their consciences and sensitivities. And it's said to be done in the name of "sensitivity."

Delegates at the 1988 General Conference felt strongly enough about this matter that they specifically instructed our bishops that when ordaining clergy, they "will use the historic language of the Holy Trinity: Father, Son, and Holy Spirit" (Par. 433, *Book of Discipline)*. Some bishops, however, simply ignore this mandate and use other language.

It's time the church faces up to the God-language controversy. What's behind much of the language crusade is, frankly, the imposition of politically correct language upon us all, to compel ideological allegiance in this symbolic way. Or in Chuck Colson's words, the real purpose is to "determine who will salute when the radical feminist flag is raised."

When words become tools imposing an ideological agenda, it is an egregious misuse of language. When this is done in the life of our church, then they have, indeed, become words that hurt and words that *heel*. When language is inducted into the murky business of indoctrination, then all of us will be the poorer for it. We expect better from the church.

Note: *Some of the more objectionable terms for the deity were removed in the final editing of the* Book of Worship. *The declining use of "Father" in United Methodist worship, however, should still be cause for concern.*

November/December 1991

"Re-Imagining" Rejects Historic Christianity

. . . .

"Most disturbing of all, many doctrines essential to orthodox Christianity were repudiated at this conference, often in a spirit of derision."

THIS issue of *Good News* carries the most disturbing news story we've ever published. It's a report on the "Re-Imagining" conference held November 4–7 in Minneapolis. Without question, this event was the most theologically aberrant I have ever read about, far removed from Christian tradition.

The Women's Division of the General Board of Global Ministries (GBGM) urged staff and directors to attend "Re-Imagining" (all expenses paid) as its theological training event for the quadrennium. Some 391 United Methodist women attended.

Having read transcripts of tapes from most presenters, I am convinced that no United Methodist women should have been subjected to this conference. Consider the following:

- Melanie Morrison, co-founder of Christian Lesbians Out Together (CLOUT), was given time to celebrate "the miracles of being lesbian, out, and Christian," and invited all other lesbian, bisexual, and transsexual women to come forward, join hands and encircle the stage. More than 100 women responded and Ms. Morrison said, "I'm pleased and honored to lead you in prayer and to talk to earth maker Mauna, our creator."
- Nadean Bishop, the first "out" lesbian minister called to an American Baptist church, said that Mary and Martha in the Bible were not actual sisters but lesbian lovers.
- "Womanist" theologian Delores S. Williams said, "I don't think we need a theory of atonement at all. . . . I don't think

we need folks hanging on crosses and blood dripping and weird stuff." Applause followed.

- Judy Westerdorf, a United Methodist clergywoman, told a workshop, "The Church has always been blessed by gays and lesbians . . . witches . . . shamans . . . artists."
- Theologian Mary Hunt said, "I have far more hope in substituting 'friendship' as a metaphor for family. . . . Imagine sex among friends as the norm, young people learning to make friends rather than to date. Imagine valuing genital sexual interaction in terms of whether and how it fosters friendship and pleasure. . . ."

The above excerpts are representative of the tone and substance of "Re-Imagining." While wading through transcripts, I counted at least ten presenters who were self-identified lesbians. Prayers were offered repeatedly to the goddess Sophia, including the offensive prayer in the "Service of milk and honey," which said, "Our sweet Sophia, we are women in your image; With nectar between our thighs we invite a lover, we birth a child."

This blending of sexuality and spirituality is more Canaanite than Christian.

Most disturbing of all, many doctrines essential to orthodox Christianity were repudiated at this conference, often in a spirit of derision. This includes the doctrine of God, the deity of Christ, his atoning death, the sinfulness of humanity, creation, the authority of Scripture, the church, and the biblical understanding of human sexuality. In a word, what was "presented" at "Re-Imagining" was a different religion.

Our United Methodist participation in such an event leaves many of us shocked and angry. Aside from being unacceptable, what does it mean? Clearly a theological polarization in the United Methodist Church is emerging. The doctrinal defection many of us have suspected from nuances and wafflings in the past has surfaced here as defiance of the historic faith.

An international gathering that publicly trashes historic Christian doctrine and celebrates sinful behavior cannot be ignored. Our United Methodist bishops must decide how they will respond to our church's participation. Is such teaching acceptable to them? If this event goes unchallenged, then the church is adrift in theological anarchy. This is not a time for dialogue, but for church discipline.

The Women's Division has betrayed its trust with the United Methodist Church. It should disavow the radical substance of this conference and apologize to the church for supporting it. But I doubt this will happen. The Women's Division knew what it was supporting.

Therefore, our United Methodist bishops must intervene. They have the specific disciplinary mandate "to guard, transmit, teach, and proclaim . . . the apostolic faith as it is expressed in Scripture and Tradition . . ." and "to teach and uphold the theological traditions of The United Methodist Church" (Par. 514.2,4). The radical nature of "Re-Imagining" makes imperative some action of theological oversight by our bishops.

In the meantime, local-church United Methodist Women (UMW) units must re-think their financial pledge support of the Women's Division if public refutation and apology are not made. Also, conference UMW leaders should call for change in the Women's Division's national leadership. Until that happens, we can only expect more of the same—or worse.

January/February 1994

Wrestling with "Re-Imagining"

*"Rather than affirming the great themes of
the Christian faith, speakers [at 'Re-
Imagining'] attacked the Church and its
doctrines as the source of oppression of
women, racism, classism,* ad infinitum.*"*

NOVEMBER'S "Re-Imagining" Conference in Minneapolis provides a painful glimpse into the theological malaise in America's mainline denominations. These churches used to be referred to as "mainstream" Protestant. This controversy, however, reminds me of the question asked by Riley Case in a *Good News* article a few years ago: "Has the Mainstream become a backyard trickle?"

Of course, the "Re-Imagining" event did *not* represent "mainstream" Protestantism or mainstream United Methodism for that matter. In fact, thousands are incensed at reports about "Re-Imagining" and will not be placated by smooth public relations efforts that gloss over or ignore the serious issues involved. Let me clarify what some of those issues are:

First, what was wrong with the "Re-Imagining" event? The conference, attended by some 2,200 participants (391 of whom were United Methodists), included: 1. prayers to and worship focused on the goddess "Sophia"; 2. derision and denial of essential Christian doctrinal tenets (incarnation, atonement, original sin, etc.); and 3. the public celebration of lesbianism. Rather than affirming the great themes of the Christian faith, speakers attacked the Church and its doctrines as the source of oppression of women, racism, classism, *ad infinitum.*

Second, what was the nature of United Methodist participation? The Women's Division of the General Board of Global Ministries took action at its spring meeting last March to cancel its own "staff and director theology workshop" and "approved" in its place involvement of staff and directors in the "Re-Imagining" event. The Women's Division has acknowledged its full financial support of 36 directors, 9 staff members, and 11 United Methodist Women (UMW) conference vice presidents, plus a grant of $2,500 in response to a request from the Minnesota Conference UMW for scholarships. This involvement clearly represents "official support" on behalf of the Women's Division.

In addition, the "Re-Imagining" program book listed several other United Methodists related to the conference. Named were Bishops Forrest C. Stith (New York) and Sharon Brown Christopher (Minnesota). Also involved as program leaders were Kathi Austin Mahle, a United Methodist clergywoman who was co-chair of the "Re-Imagining" steering committee, and Jeanne Audrey Powers, associate general secretary of the General Commission on Christian Unity and Interreligious Concerns, who also served on the steering committee. Ms. Mahle and Ms. Powers would no doubt have been involved in the planning of the event. All this represents significant United Methodist involvement in both planning and participation.

Third, didn't the Women's Division "Fact Sheet" and "video letter" adequately explain its involvement in the conference? Quite simply, no. Neither the "Fact Sheet" nor the video provided substantive or satisfactory answers. Trying to calm the storm, the Women's Division has asked innocently, "Do United Methodist Women have the ability to evaluate information they hear when presented with new, diverse views?" But what were these "new, diverse views"? They were not subtle nuances or fresh insights about biblical truth. They were radical departures from historic Christian doctrine and teaching.

At "Re-Imagining," Sophia was center stage. The entire gathering prayed to her, blessed every speaker in her name, and joined in the highly-offensive "Milk and Honey" service on the final day. One clergywoman who attended told a conference edition of *The United Methodist Reporter:* "This was the first time I had encountered Sophia worship or praying in the name of Sophia or invoking the spirit of Sophia."

What distresses many of us is that after three months, the Women's Division has expressed no regret or reservations whatsoever about the offensive content of the conference. Some of their comments have even seemed intentionally evasive.

This controversy reflects the theological crisis already present within United Methodism. We don't all need to walk in theological lock-step. But we do need to walk within the boundaries of classical Christianity—respectful of that which has always, everywhere, and by all Christians been believed about God.

By now United Methodist bishops have transcripts of enough of the questionable content of "Re-Imagining" to know there were serious substantive problems with it. The Good News board took action at its January meeting to ask the Council of Bishops to address this theological crisis. The Council should assure anxious United Methodists, in no uncertain terms, that the substance of the "Re-Imagining" conference was, indeed, unacceptable in terms of our United Methodist theological tradition. The church needs a clear response from its episcopal leaders.

March/April 1994

The Hope for a New Reformation

. . . .

"(Richard) Lovelace believes, in fact, that all the mainline denominations in America are on the edge of a major and long-overdue Reformation in the scriptural sense, and that the furor from 'Re-Imagining' could well be the catalyst that helps bring it about."

AFTER six turbulent months of controversy following the "Re-Imagining" Conference, the United Methodist bishops discussed the issue at their May meeting and authorized a task force to perform a six-month study on the concept of "wisdom" in the Old and New Testaments.

This action is insufficient and ignores a host of disturbing, but persistent, questions about "Re-Imagining" that still remain unaddressed. Prayers and liturgies to the goddess "Sophia" were only a portion of many irregularities at the event. But they were, nonetheless, a serious problem.

Some participants claim that they were not talking about a "goddess" at the conference. However, that claim is easily overruled. The daily "Re-Imagining" Conference newsletter included teachings from *Wisdom's Feast,* a book about "Sophia" authored in part by United Methodist pastors Susan Cady and Hal Taussig. In that work, the authors are clear in their description of "Sophia" as a goddess: "For most of us, thinking about God in the language and configuration of the goddess means a monumental shift" (p. 165). And, "We must find a way to mainstream the goddess into the universe within which women are actually living their lives" (p. 10).

By its action and subsequent comments, the Council of Bishops has said in effect that it does not see the "Re-Imagining" event as a serious concern in the life of our church. Though several bishops had written previously that Sophia's intrusion into Christian worship is, indeed, heresy (a strong charge), the Council in its official action chose to avoid any negative statement about the conference.

While our UM bishops downplayed the crisis, a reporter on ABC's *Nightline* program (May 24) noted that the "Re-Imagining" event had unleashed "the ecumenical equivalent of an earthquake." Rita Nakashima Brock, a "Re-Imagining" speaker who appeared on *Nightline*, acknowledged that the feminist theology is "re-examining every central tenet of Christian faith—both for their male dominance and for the harm that they do to women, and *reconceiving them*" (emphasis added). Don't miss that. They are "reconceiving" every "central tenet" of Christian faith.

Presbyterians continue to feel the aftershocks of this ecumenical earthquake. Some 50 percent of all the "overtures" [petitions] to the recent Presbyterian Church (USA) annual assembly dealt with the "Re-Imagining" event. So great has been the furor that Mary Ann Lundy, a high-level executive, was forced to resign her position. The Presbyterians have acknowledged they will lose at least $4 million (some say maybe $8 to $12 million) by the time it's over. Not long ago I received a call from Dr. Richard Lovelace, professor of church history at Gordon-Conwell Theological Seminary. Lovelace is a respected Presbyterian theologian who has regularly attended meetings of the World Council of Churches. An incurable optimist, he always sees the Holy Spirit at work somewhere in the WCC. When he called, he had just listened to three-fourths of the 24 tapes from "Re-Imagining" and would soon finish the rest. In a sobered tone, he said, "Jim, that conference was worse than the media has reported. Frankly, I'm frightened. They threw the scriptural God out the window."

In the most recent issue of *The Presbyterian Layman*, Lovelace wrote, "Average Presbyterians who listen to the 24 tapes . . . cannot believe that this sort of teaching is happening in their church. They are also stunned by the fact that Presbyterian staff persons helped design the conference . . . and . . . are baffled by the refusal of the church's central leadership to admit and repudiate the church's participation in this attack on its own historic faith."

Lovelace also observed that the "predominance of Liberalism," which has grown in the Presbyterian Church since the 1920s, "is about to collapse." He adds, "What is needed is for conservative and center-church leaders to work together to construct a viable future for the church. Such a coalition is possible, and there are signs that . . . this is exactly what is happening."

In United Methodism this may have been happening via the Houston and Memphis Declarations, or more recently, the Atlanta "Invitation to the Church" [from the initial meeting that led to the formation of the Confessing Movement Within the United Methodist Church]. Lovelace believes, in fact, that all the mainline denominations in America are on the edge of a major and long overdue Reformation in the scriptural sense, and that the furor from "Re-Imagining" could well be the catalyst that helps bring it about. I believe this is a real possibility for United Methodists, who remain shocked about "Re-Imagining" and will no longer tolerate such careless handling of "the faith which was once for all delivered to the saints" (Jude 3, RSV).

Let's covenant together to pray daily for such a Reformation.

July/August 1994

Reaffirming the Centrality of Christ

. . . .

"Calling the church to reaffirm the centrality of Jesus is like having the American Medical Association reaffirm medication and surgery. The very thought seems ludicrous."

AT its annual winter meeting (January 1995), the Good News board of directors took two actions addressing the theological crisis in the United Methodist Church: It called upon the church *to reaffirm* the centrality of Jesus Christ, including his incarnation, deity, and atoning death for sin; and it expressed *deep concern* about the recent formation of a "Re-Imagining Community," headquartered in Minneapolis.

Calling the church to reaffirm the centrality of Jesus is like having the American Medical Association reaffirm medication and surgery. The very thought seems ludicrous. The truth is, however, that United Methodism remains on shaky theological soil in its understanding and teaching about Jesus Christ.

Following the 1993 "Re-Imagining" Conference at which the uniqueness, deity, and atoning death of Jesus were denied and the goddess "Sophia" worshiped, some 830 United Methodist women in various leadership positions signed a statement entitled, "A Time of Hope—A Time of Threat." It charged that those of us disagreeing with the substance of "Re-Imagining" were "frightened by fresh theological insights and by challenges to [our] narrow orthodoxy," and that we were "attempting to discredit and malign women." What is happening, the statement said, is a "revolution," and it called on all to "join us in celebrating and living into this *movement* of the Holy Spirit" (emphasis mine).

This past October 29 a "Re-Imagining" reunion was held in Minneapolis. Participants announced the formation of an ongoing "Re-Imagining Community" with tax-exempt status. A United Methodist elder and a national United Methodist program staff person serve as members of the coordinating council of the new entity. At the reunion, Rita Nakashima Brock, professor at United Methodist-related Hamline University and speaker at the first "Re-Imagining" meeting, was the only plenary speaker. Brock negated, by a volley of rhetorical questions, the traditional understanding of atonement and went on to claim that the incarnation was an "ongoing process," rather than an event that occurred "once for all" in Jesus of Nazareth. She added, "We give a moment of honor to Jesus for what he did—but others must come after." To affirm this, of course, means one cannot say, "You are the Christ, the Son of the living God" (Matthew 16:16).

United Methodists, who continue to discuss the controversy, could learn much from the Presbyterian Church (USA), whose General Assembly met last spring amidst talk of a possible split because of "Re-Imagining." But chaos was avoided. Why? Because the Assembly admitted that "Re-Imagining" constituted "a theological crisis." Delegates acknowledged that "some of the theological content . . . and worship rituals not only extended beyond boundaries of the Reformed theological tradition but also beyond that tradition's understanding of what makes faith Christian." The Assembly also admitted that the conference "used language, including the term 'sophia,' in ways that imply worship of a divine manifestation distinctly different from 'the one triune God.'"

Prior to the Presbyterian Assembly, six professors at Princeton Theological Seminary drafted and signed "An Open Letter to Presbyterians," a sophisticated theological analysis of the conference. Their letter reminds us that truth alone is the only basis for unity in the church. It says, "The unity of the church is not endangered where heresies are labeled as such . . . It is not those who point out the heresy and apostasy of others who break the unity. It is rather the heretic and the apostate who break the unity of the church by undermining the church's obedience to its Head. Those who raise the necessary protest are simply bringing to the light of day the fact that the unity of the Church has already been shattered." Well said.

The Princeton theologians then gave "Re-Imagining" this stunning indictment: "Given the pervasive affirmation of a multiplicity of incarnations and the marginalization of Jesus which accompanied it, the only possible conclusion is that the worship of 'Sophia' was the worship of a deity which is other than and alien to the God incarnate in Jesus Christ. . . . Therefore, it will not do, as some have attempted . . . to say that the worship of 'Sophia' which occurred there was the worship of Jesus Christ by another name. No, the 'Sophia' worshipped in Minneapolis was a god other than the God who was incarnate in Jesus Christ. The 'Sophia' worshipped in Minneapolis was a false god."

United Methodists remain uneasy that their church seems uncertain about who Jesus is. We need the kind of candid critique that these theologians provided for the Presbyterian Church. Better to face up to theological error than to conceal it and continue boasting about our grand diversity.

March/April 1995

The Subversion of the Church

. . . .

*"Of course, once one accepts that the
Christian faith is a human invention, or
that revelation continues to happen today
through women's experience, one is not
far from denying the uniqueness and
deity of Jesus."*

ONE of the memorable moments of the Theological Dialogue in Nashville last November was hearing a poignant statement from Mary Daffin, an African-American attorney from Houston. She confessed to being stunned by what she had heard in her small group session. She said, "The things I've heard have been very disturbing. I have no theology degrees. I don't know all the doctrines. But I come from a heritage where all we have is Jesus. I don't want to hear that my church doesn't believe in that Jesus. I know what Scripture says about certain things. I believe in it. I accept and love others, but I can't depart from Scriptures, and I believe in their authority."

Mary, a member of the Steering Committee of the Confessing Movement within the United Methodist Church, sensed that some folks were doing violence to the traditional teachings of her church.

Another organization concerned about fidelity to the Scriptures has appeared on the national scene, and United Methodists need to know about it. In late 1993, the Ecumenical Coalition on Women and Society (ECWS) was launched, as a project of the Institute on Religion and Democracy (IRD).

ECWS has taken the lead in an effort to call women within mainline denominations to affirm a positive Christian alternative to radical feminist ideology. Last September, ECWS issued, "A Christian Women's Declaration," an impressive, pro-active statement for Christian women.

Just two months after releasing its Declaration, the ECWS sponsored its "Washington Summit '97," held in Washington, D.C. More than 100 articulate, persuasive orthodox Christian spokeswomen gathered to learn how they might better counter the arguments of secular feminists and influence the ongoing debate over the role of women in our churches and in American society.

In her panel address at the event, Donna F. G. Hailson, professor at Gordon-Conwell Theological Seminary and an active participant in American Baptist Evangelicals, spoke on "The Undermining of the Church." She reported that one of the themes of the 1996 Re-Imagining Reunion Conference was "Ecclesial Subversion." *Subversion,* she noted, is defined as the attempt to overthrow, undermine, or completely destroy. Ecclesial, of course, refers to the church. She reminded participants that the Re-Imagining Community is subversive, starting with the assumption that since men "imagined" God and the teachings of the Christian faith, it is now the right and even the responsibility of women (primarily) to do some re-imagining, some undermining, some subverting of this faith. (Another Re-Imagining Reunion is set for this April [1998] in St. Paul, Minnesota.)

Of course, once one accepts that the Christian faith is a human invention, or that revelation continues to happen today through women's experience, one is not far from denying the uniqueness and deity of Jesus. He is reduced to merely a good example, "an important and powerful ancestor," but he is rejected as God incarnate.

It is this kind of aberrant theology that "A Christian Women's Declaration" addresses. In the opening sentence, the women declare "First and foremost, we are women of faith and principle whose Christianity is founded not on human invention but on divinely revealed truth." They insist they are "beneficiaries, not victims," of the Christian faith. The Bible has not been oppressive, but a "liberating force." It has been the most effective force in history "for lifting women to higher levels of respect, dignity, and freedom."

In a section of Affirmations, the Declaration affirms the triune God, the authority of the Scriptures, the natural created order, and human sinfulness. Concerning the latter, the women affirm, "We acknowledge ourselves to be sinners—without the resources within ourselves to know or to serve God adequately."

In the section of "Challenges" facing Christian women today, a major concern is with "Radical Feminism," a movement whose agenda has "revolutionary, not reformist, goals." The evangelical women reject the portrayal of women as "victims," the exaggerations of women's suffering, and the denial that advances have been made in recognition of women's rights.

Radical Feminism is seen to be "undermining" the Christian churches. The statement expresses concern about "The movement to 're-imagine' two thousand years of Christian faith." It is troubled also by "the movement to reject any objective ultimate authority and elevate human experience as the only source of meaning."

The declaration has been endorsed by a number of prominent Christian women, including Elizabeth Achtemeier, Mary Ellen Bork, Janice Shaw Crouse, Helen Hull Hitchcock, Diane Knippers, Faye Short, Helen Rhea Stumbo, and Charmaine Crouse Yoest, to name just a few.

This declaration is a timely and theologically-sound response to the agenda of Radical Feminism—an agenda which, we must remember, seeks "ecclesial subversion." This statement merits careful reading and study across the church, by both women and men. For a copy of the statement, write to: ECWS, 1521 Sixteenth St., NW, Suite 300, Washington, D.C. 20036; phone (202) 986-1440.

March/April 1998

Appendixes

Introduction

ONE of the impressive realities of the last decade is how evangelicals, United Methodists and others, have gathered out of concern about the doctrinal and moral problems facing their churches. These concerned United Methodists have issued statements or declarations on behalf of the evangelical and traditional constituencies of their churches. What follows are six of those statements or declarations, most of which have been alluded to earlier in this book. Together, they represent an important call to the church and its leaders to be faithful to the historic doctrines and moral standards of the church.

Appendix I:
The Houston Declaration

In December of 1987, 48 leading United Methodist ministers from 42 churches in 18 states gathered in Houston to draft a strongly worded statement cautioning the United Methodist Church against a move away from traditional doctrine.

The pastors from some of the denomination's largest churches came on short notice and at their own expense at the invitation of seven prominent United Methodist pastors, including William H. Hinson, pastor of Houston's First United Methodist Church, who served as chairman of the group and host pastor for the gathering.

On December 15, the organizing pastors released "The Houston Declaration" to the media, a document carefully prepared by those present which affirmed their strong support of three key United Methodist positions: (1) The primacy of Scripture; (2) The traditional language of the Holy Trinity as "Father, Son and Holy Spirit"; and (3) The ban against the ordination of those persons practicing homosexuality.

In addition to Hinson, the other pastors who signed the letter of invitation for the gathering included: James Buskirk, pastor of First UMC in Tulsa; Maxie Dunnam, pastor of Christ UMC in Memphis; Ira Gallaway, pastor of First UMC in Peoria, J. Ellsworth Kalas, pastor of Church of the Savior in Cleveland; John Ed Mathison, pastor of Frazier Memorial UMC in Montgomery; and Gerald Trigg, pastor of First UMC in Colorado Springs.

What did they think might result from the gathering and statement? Dr. Ira Gallaway, one of the key organizing pastors, said he believed the meeting will cause other United

Methodist clergy and laity to stand up and be counted. "We are sounding a clear note for people to rally around and take hope in," said Gallaway.

All 48 clergy present signed the Houston Declaration.

* * * * *

THE HOUSTON DECLARATION

OUT of love and concern for the United Methodist Church, 48 pastors from 18 states, from Massachusetts to California, from Illinois to Florida, representing large churches and small, came together in Houston, Texas, December 14–15, 1987. We came as pastors who baptize and marry, confirm and bury and live among our people. We came to reaffirm and promote the central certainties of our faith. In the face of actions by some boards and agencies and some caucus groups that tend to undermine these certainties, and in the fulfillment of our ordination vows, we feel compelled to speak to three crucial truths which are essential to the life, witness and scriptural integrity of the church: (1) the primacy of Scripture; (2) the nature and name of the one God, Father, Son, and Holy Spirit; and (3) the high and holy character of ordained ministry.

I. THE PRIMACY OF SCRIPTURE

We United Methodist pastors affirm the Wesleyan principle of the primacy of Scripture and recognize that we share a common heritage with Christians of every age and nation. We have witnessed the confusion and conflict resulting from the ambiguity of the present doctrinal statement as contained in Paragraph 69 of the 1984 *Discipline.*

We therefore endorse the following declaration regarding the primacy of Scripture, as included in the newly proposed doctrinal statement:

United Methodists share with other Christians the conviction that Scripture is the primary source and criterion for authentic Christian truth and witness. The Bible bears authoritative testimony to God's self-disclosure in the pilgrimage of Israel, in the life, death, and resurrection of Jesus Christ, and in the Holy Spirit's constant activity in human history, especially in the mission of early Christianity. As we open our minds and hearts to the Word of God through the words of human beings inspired by the Holy Spirit, faith is born and nourished, our understanding is deepened, and the possibilities for transforming the world become apparent to us.

The Bible is sacred canon for Christian people, formally acknowledged as such by historic ecumenical councils of the church. Our doctrinal standards identify as canonical thirty-nine books of the Old Testament and the twenty-seven books of the New Testament. Our standards affirm the Bible as the source of all that is "necessary and sufficient unto salvation" (Articles of Religion) and "the true rule and guide for faith and practice" (Confession of Faith).

We properly read Scripture within the believing community, informed by the tradition of that community. We interpret individual texts in light of their place in the Bible as a whole. We are aided by scholarly inquiry and personal insight, under the guidance of the Holy Spirit. Wesley's method of interpretation applied this rule: "The obscure text is to be interpreted by those which speak more plainly," and the more difficult passages understood in terms of the "analogy of faith," that is, "the whole scope and tenor of Scripture," the core witness of Scripture as a whole . . . The Bible serves both as a source of our faith and as the basic criterion by which the truth and fidelity of any interpretation of faith is measured.

II. THE TRINITY

We confess the historic Christian Faith in the one God, Father, Son, and Holy Spirit.

In Jesus Christ, the divine Son, God has been definitively revealed to humankind, and the world graciously reconciled to God. At the exaltation of Jesus, the one whom he consistently called Father sent forth the Holy Spirit to declare the things of Christ, so that the good news of our redemption might be proclaimed to all people. At least since the gospel of St. Matthew, the church has consistently baptized "in the name of the Father, the Son, and the Holy Spirit" those who accept the message (Matthew 28:19–20).

We deplore the effort in baptism, ordination, and the total liturgy of the Church to resymbolize the Faith by abandoning the name of God, Father, Son and Holy Spirit or adopting inadequate substitutes. To do so is to deny the revelation attested in the Scriptures, transmitted by faithful men and women in the Christian tradition, and offered to the world for its salvation.

Formulas such as "Creator, Redeemer, Sustainer" or "Creator, Christ, Spirit" are inadequate substitutes. As to the first: God's richly personal being cannot be defined merely in functional terms. As to the second: Christ and the Spirit are not mere creatures.

We affirm equality and inclusive language in all human relationships.

III. THE ORDAINED MINISTRY

The Church, on the authority of the Scriptures, has never viewed homosexuality as a part of God's diverse, good creation, but has always considered homosexual practices as a sin and a manifestation of the brokenness of God's fallen creation. Every scriptural reference to the practice of homosexuality is negative (Leviticus 18:22; 20:13; Romans 1:18–32; 1 Corinthians 6:9–10). Following the Old Testament prohibitions, the apostle Paul sees homosexual practices as the sign and consequence of a turning away from the Creator in order to worship the creature. Homosexual practices become an extreme expression of the turning in upon itself which is the essence of humankind's sin.

We repudiate all irrational fear of and contempt for homosexual persons. We affirm a ministry of Christian compassion, care and redirection for those who have engaged in homosexual practices as they seek help in overcoming temptation and changing their style of life. Persons may or may not be able to change their sexual orientation; persons can change their lifestyle. That possibility is the very essence of the gospel of Christ (1 Corinthians 6).

It is not acceptable in the context of the Christian faith that persons engaging in homosexual practices should be ordained to the ministry or continue in representative positions within the Church.

CONCLUSION

We covenant together to proclaim these central truths of the Christian Faith and to invest our lives and ministry in the continuing renewal of our beloved Church. We invite all, laity and clergy of the United Methodist Church, to join with us as persons who have been called to follow Christ and give our lives to advancing the gospel and the historic Christian Faith. The need is urgent—the time is now!

We stand as servants and disciples of Jesus Christ our Lord.

ORGANIZING MINISTERS

Rev. James B. Buskirk, First United Methodist Church, Tulsa, OK

Rev. Maxie D. Dunnam, Christ United Methodist Church, Memphis, TN

Rev. Ira Gallaway, First United Methodist Church, Peoria, IL

Rev. William H. Hinson, First United Methodist Church, Houston, TX

Rev. J. Ellsworth Kalas, The Church of the Savior, Cleveland, OH

Rev. John Ed Mathison, Frazer Memorial United Methodist Church, Montgomery, AL

Rev. O. Gerald Trigg, First United Methodist Church, Colorado Springs, CO

SIGNATORIES TO THE DECLARATION

Rev. Barbara Brokhoff, Evangelist, Clearwater, FL

Rev. Joseph H. Bullington, Jr., Cokesbury UMC, Pensacola, FL

Rev. Kirbyjon Caldwell, Windsor Village UMC, Houston, TX

Rev. Riley Case, District Superintendent, Marion, IN

Rev. Brad Dinsmore, Lake Magdalene UMC, Tampa, FL

Rev. Malone Dodson, Roswell UMC, Roswell, GA

Rev. Roy Dunn, Good Samaritan UMC, Cupertino, CA

Rev. P. Jackson Edwards, Wesley Memorial UMC, Cleveland, TN

Rev. Thomas E. Farmer, First UMC, Jacksonville, FL

Rev. Larry Goodpaster, Oxford University UMC, Oxford, MS

Rev. C.W. Hancock, District Superintendent, Macon, GA

Rev. Don Harp, Gainesville UMC, Gainesville, GA

Rev. Carl Harris, St. Paul's UMC, Orangeburg, SC

Rev. Cornelius Henderson, District Superintendent, Atlanta, GA

Rev. J. William Hones, Grace UMC, Decatur, IL

Rev. Jimmy Jones, First UMC, Orlando, FL

Rev. William R. Key, Isle of Hope UMC, Savannah, GA

Rev. R.L. Kirk, St. Luke's UMC, Lubbock, TX

Rev. Arthur Landwehr, First UMC, Evanston, IL

Rev. J.R. McCormick, Parkway Heights UMC, Hattiesburg, MS

Rev. Henry Matthews, Bon Air UMC, Richmond, VA

Rev. William Morris, District Superintendent, Murfreesboro, TN

Rev. Raymond Owen, First UMC, Bartlesville, OK

Rev. John Patterson, Grace UMC, Indiana, PA

Rev. Ora Bell Peck, Bardwell UMC, Bardwell, KY

Rev. William Pickett, Pine Castle UMC, Orlando, FL

Rev. Joe A. Rand, People's UMC, Bradford, MA

Rev. Richard Rohrer, Hyde Park UMC, Tampa, FL

Rev. William W. Roughton, First UMC, Melbourne, FL

Rev. Charles Sayre, Haddonfield UMC, Haddonfield, NJ

Rev. David Seamands, Asbury Theological Seminary, Wilmore, KY

Rev. Charles Sineath, First UMC, Marietta, GA

Rev. Robert Snyder, First UMC, Cardington, OH

Rev. Robert Souders, St. Matthew's UMC, Belleville, IL

Rev. Robert H. Spain, Brentwood UMC, Brentwood, TN

Rev. Edd Templeton, First UMC, Tullahoma, TN

Rev. Vernon Tyson, Edenton Street UMC, Raleigh, NC

Rev. Al Vom Steeg, St. Luke's UMC, Fresno, CA

Rev. Charles D. Whittle, First UMC, Abilene, TX

Rev. Garnett Wilder, Snellville UMC, Snellville, GA

Rev. Charles W. Williams, Moody Memorial First UMC, Galveston, TX

Rev. Ruth M. Wood, Byhalia UMC, Byhalia, MS

Rev. E.R. Woolridge, Jr., Virginia Beach UMC, Virginia Beach, VA

Appendix II: A Call to Action

On February 27-28, 1988, some 47 lay persons representing all jurisdictions of the United Methodist Church gathered in Chicago to support the Houston Declaration, believing it was time to issue a call to action. These lay persons believed that action in support of the Houston Declaration would help thrust their church to renewed effectiveness and spiritual power equal to the challenges of the day. They also affirmed support for church legislation that would make clear the basics of the faith as outlined in the Declaration.

The Steering Committee members for the Call To Action included the following United Methodist lay persons: Mr. David Dolsen, lay delegate, Rocky Mountain Conference; Mrs. June Parker Goldman, Lay Delegate, Iowa Conference; Mr. Gus Gustafson, Lay Delegate, North Georgia Conference; Dr. Jim Holsinger, Leader, Lay Delegation, Virginia Conference; Mrs. Eve Kirk, Lay Delegate, Northern Illinois Conference; Mrs. June D. McCullough, Chair, Southern New Jersey Delegation; and Mr. William Randolph Smith, Lay Delegate, Texas Conference.

* * * * *

A CALL TO ACTION

A LAY RESPONSE TO THE HOUSTON DECLARATION

We, as concerned laity from every jurisdiction of the United Methodist Church, gathered in Chicago, Illinois, February 27-28, 1988, to support the Houston Declaration. At this time the issues addressed by this Declaration—the primacy of

Scripture, the nature and name of the Trinity, and the character of the ordained ministry—are critical in the life of our church. Efforts to deviate from these historic principles violate our beliefs as United Methodist laity. It is for this reason that we have met and developed this document.

THE PRIMACY OF SCRIPTURE

We, as laity, welcome and endorse the Houston Declaration's clear statement on the primacy of Scripture. John Wesley declared that he was a man of one Book. It is clear from his life and words that John Wesley believed in and practiced a life that was rooted in the primacy of Scripture. Here we use the term primacy to mean in first place. We believe that Scripture is the basis for our faith and practice of Christianity. Without Scripture there would be no Christianity as we know it, since there would be no written revelation by God to the people of the world. Reason, tradition, and experience, under the guidance of the Holy Spirit, assist in the interpretation of the Scripture for every time and age. We find the primacy of Scripture to be within the traditions of Wesleyan Christianity. We stand fully committed to the primacy of Scripture as the basis of our Christian faith and practice.

THE TRINITY

We, as laity, appreciate and support the Houston Declaration's statement regarding the Trinity. We affirm the traditional names of "Father, Son, and Holy Spirit" for the Trinity. Jesus himself instructed us to baptize in the name of the Father, Son, and Holy Spirit. We believe that for ordination and the sacraments of the Church, Baptism and Communion, these names cannot be improved upon. We further believe we are invoking the power and blessings of God by using the names of the Father, Son, and Holy Spirit in our worship experience. We must guard against language that would devalue the Trinity and weaken our faith. God desires a personal relationship with us, and to substitute functional words does not adequately convey this relationship.

THE ORDAINED MINISTRY

We, as laity, affirm the high character of ordained ministry and the historic Christian stand on the sin of homosexual practice as stated in the Houston Declaration. The Church, on the authority of Scripture, has set high standards for ordained ministry. We call upon Conference Boards of Ordained Ministry to maintain these high standards and uphold the *Discipline*. Although we support the United Methodist Church position on chargeable offenses (Par. 2621), we strongly urge action by the 1988 General Conference to strengthen and clarify standards for ordained individuals. We reaffirm the traditional Christian standard of sexual morality; celibacy in singleness and fidelity in marriage. We believe it is not acceptable in the context of the Christian faith that persons unwilling to maintain these high standards be accepted as candidates, ordained as ministers, or appointed to serve in the United Methodist Church. We affirm a ministry of Christian compassion, care, and redirection for clergy who have not maintained the standards set by the church.

A CALL TO ACTION

Let us respond now to the Houston Declaration in a spirit of prayer, hope, love, and commitment to our historic Christian Faith. For too long too many of us have remained silent, deeply concerned about the decline of our Church but uncertain what we should do. Now it is time for every concerned United Methodist to speak and act positively, while loving and respecting those who disagree with us.

We call on every United Methodist layperson who wants a vital, renewed, Christ-centered church to speak out now for the Houston Declaration and its principles. We invite laypersons to endorse this Laity Response. There is a great need for each person to state his or her views to pastors, delegates, members of Annual Conferences, bishops, and church agencies.

We call on every United Methodist pastor to present the Houston Declaration to his or her congregation, invite their study and response, and give an opportunity to sign an endorsement of the Houston Declaration.

We call on every local church Administrative Board or Council to endorse the Houston Declaration and send this endorsement to General and Jurisdictional Conference delegates.

We call on all delegates to the 1988 General and Jurisdictional Conferences and all members of Annual Conferences to take action and adopt specific legislation upholding the principles of the Houston Declaration.

We call on all United Methodists to make a personal commitment to join us in earnest prayer for the General Conference and its delegates during each day of the General Conference.

We believe the Holy Spirit speaks to us through the courageous pastors who wrote and signed the Houston Declaration. We believe the Holy Spirit now calls us to give our active support and help our church to be faithful to God's Word and our Wesleyan heritage.

This we do in the name of our Lord Jesus Christ.

Chicago, Illinois
February 28, 1988

Appendix III:
The DuPage Declaration

In March of 1990, a coalition of 21 evangelical renewal leaders from eight denominations drafted the DuPage Declaration: A Call to Biblical Fidelity. The document affirmed important theological and ethical standards that were under challenge in their respective communions.

The document was shaped and adopted by evangelical Renewal Executives during a two-day consultation held at Wheaton College. The Renewal Executives had been meeting annually for 13 years to share experiences in the realm of spiritual renewal in their own particular branch of the Church of Jesus Christ. The Rev. James V. Heidinger II, executive secretary of Good News, moderated the two day session that produced the Declaration. Discussion had begun several years earlier about the possibility of creating a document that would express the biblically based convictions and concerns of the entire group. Dr. Donald Bloesch, professor at Dubuque Theological Seminary, wrote the first draft of the declaration.

The DuPage Declaration was a clarion call to the entire Church of Jesus Christ expressing concern about the Church's drift away from the evangelical faith. It was entitled "The DuPage Declaration" because it was a statement finalized while the Renewal Executives were meeting in Wheaton, Illinois, which is located in DuPage County.

Asked whether the Declaration might further polarize denominations that are already suffering membership losses, the signers of the document said they hope their words could help restore health and vigor, especially to historic Protestant communions.

In October, 1996, the Renewal Executives formed what is now known as the Association for Church Renewal. The Association meets semi-annually.

* * * * *

THE DUPAGE DECLARATION

. . . .

A CALL TO BIBLICAL FIDELITY

. . . .

PREAMBLE

We evangelical renewal leaders from North American mainline churches gathered at Wheaton in DuPage County, Illinois, March 19-20, 1990, express our concern for the Church of Jesus Christ in its drift away from the evangelical faith. What is needed, we believe, is a genuine revival rooted in the Word of God. We, therefore, present this declaration: *A Call to Biblical Fidelity.*

This declaration represents our understanding of theological and moral issues that are now in dispute in our churches. It is not intended to be an exhaustive list of church doctrines and concerns.

It is offered in the spirit of Christ, our Savior and Judge, who calls each of us to confess our complicity in private and public sin, "For it is time for judgment to begin with the family of God" (1 Peter 4:17, NIV; cf. 2 Timothy 4:1–5). We resolve to serve Him with total fidelity and obedience to His Word.

DECLARATION

I

WE AFFIRM the Trinitarian name of God—Father, Son and Holy Spirit.

WE DENY that these designations are mere metaphors drawn from the cultural experience of the past and may therefore be replaced by new symbols reflecting the cultural ethos of today.

II

WE AFFIRM that God has revealed himself fully and decisively in Jesus Christ as attested in Holy Scripture.

WE DENY that there are other revelations in nature or history that fulfill or complete this one revelation of God.

III

WE AFFIRM that there is only one way to salvation—God's way to us in Jesus Christ, which is apprehended by faith alone through God's grace.

WE DENY that other religions are pathways to salvation, or that one can be in a right relationship with God apart from repentance and faith in Jesus Christ.

IV

WE AFFIRM that Jesus Christ is God incarnate in human flesh, fully human and fully divine, different from all other human beings in kind, not simply in degree.

WE DENY that Jesus Christ is essentially the flower of humanity, a spiritual master, a paradigm of what all human beings can become.

V

WE AFFIRM that Holy Scripture is the written Word of God, the uniquely inspired testimony to God's self-disclosure in the history of biblical Israel culminating in Jesus Christ. The scriptures of the Old and New Testaments take precedence over experience, tradition and reason and are therefore our infallible standard for faith and practice.

WE DENY that Holy Scripture is a merely human document that records the religious experiences of a past people, that it is only an aid in understanding our experiences in the present rather than a rule that is used by the Spirit of God to direct the people of God in every age.

VI

WE AFFIRM the biblical guidelines for human sexuality: chastity outside of marriage, lifelong fidelity and holiness in marriage, and celibacy for the sake of the kingdom.

WE DENY that premarital or extramarital relations, trial marriages, cohabitation outside of marriage, homosexual relations and so-called homosexual unions, can ever be in genuine accord with the will and purpose of God for his people.

VII

WE AFFIRM the sanctity of human life at every stage based on our creation in the image of God and our election by God for service in his kingdom.

WE DENY, for example, that the personal choice of either parent takes precedence over the right of the unborn child to life in the service of God's glory. We deplore the continuing traffic of abortion as the slaughter of innocents, which can only be an abomination in the sight of God.

VIII

WE AFFIRM that the mission of the church is to spread the good news of salvation by word and deed to a lost and despairing humanity. This mission to proclaim the atoning death and resurrection of Jesus Christ to all nations calls people of faith to discipleship and obedience in the pursuit of personal and social holiness. We further affirm that the fruit of the gospel proclamation is justice, mercy and peace.

WE DENY that the mission of the church is the self-development of exploited peoples or the political liberation of oppressed peoples.

We invite pastors and laypeople from the body of Christ to join us in affirming this declaration.

ORIGINAL SIGNATORIES

Timothy Bayly, Presbyterian Church (USA)

Donald G. Bloesch, United Church of Christ

Richard M. Bowman, Christian Church (Disciples of Christ)

Ray Bringham, Church of God, Anderson

J. Robert Campbell, Presbyterian Church (USA)

James V. Heidinger II, United Methodist Church

David M. Higbee, Independent Evangelical

Paul D. Johnston, Presbyterian Church (USA)

James Mark Kushiner, Independent Evangelical

Brad Long, Presbyterian Church (USA)

Richard Lovelace, Presbyterian Church (USA)

Billy Melvin, National Association of Evangelicals

Betty Moore, Presbyterian Church (USA)

Kevin Perrotta, Roman Catholic

Kevin D. Ray, Christian Church (Disciples of Christ)

Gerald M. Sanders, United Church of Christ

Vernon Stoop, Jr., United Church of Christ

Armand L. Weller, United Church of Christ

Matthew J. Welde, Presbyterian Church (USA)

Waldo Werning, Lutheran (Missouri Synod)

Todd Wetzel, Episcopal Church

Appendix IV:
The Louisville Declaration

In July of 1990, nearly 1,000 persons gathered at the Galt House Hotel in Louisville, Kentucky, for the Convocation on World Mission and Evangelism. The event was sponsored jointly by Good News, The Mission Society for United Methodists, A Foundation for Theological Education and the National Association of United Methodist Evangelists.

Speakers at the national gathering included Bishop Richard B. Wilke, Bishop William R. Cannon, Bishop Earl G. Hunt, Jr., Nigerian Bishop Ayo Ladigbolu, Dr. Ira Gallaway, Dr. Gerald Anderson, Dr. Walter Kimbrough, Dr. William Hinson, Dr. George G. Hunter III, Mrs. Julia McClean Williams, Dr. Geoffrey Wainwright (paper read by Dr. H.T. Maclin), and Dr. Ed Robb.

On the final morning of the convocation, participants were invited to stand, expressing their support by consensus of a statement that had been prepared and distributed the previous evening for reflection and feedback. The statement, called "The Louisville Declaration—A Call to Faithfulness in Mission" was drafted by a small committee, chaired by Dr. Dean Gilliland, director of the Cross-Cultural Studies Program and professor of contextualized theology and African studies at Fuller Theological Seminary.

The Louisville Declaration invited those present to join in embracing several concerns, which include in part: 1) to reaffirm that Jesus Christ is the only Savior of people everywhere; 2) to renew dedication to the evangelization of the world; 3) to evangelize children and youth; 4) to recognize that at the heart of our church's crisis is a defection from her *essential Wesleyan doctrine; and 5) to pray for a bold new leadership in the church.*

* * * * *

THE LOUISVILLE DECLARATION

A CALL TO FAITHFULNESS IN MISSION

PREAMBLE

We have gathered in Louisville as United Methodists from thirty-eight states to reaffirm the Great Commission and to renew our vision for spreading the Gospel of Christ at home and abroad. Throughout the convocation we have rejoiced in our oneness and have faced our failures. In a spirit of repentance, we invite United Methodists to join us in embracing the following concerns:

I

We reaffirm that Jesus Christ is the only Savior of people everywhere, regardless of birth or religion. Jesus said, "Unless you are converted and become like children, you will never enter the Kingdom of Heaven" (Matthew 18:3). Today, when people of all religions live in close contact with each other, we must declare that the pre-eminent Christ is above any religious or social system. This leads us to work for the conversion of the nations as our Lord commanded (Matthew 28:19).

II

We dedicate ourselves anew to the evangelization of the world, praying that God would enhance our zeal for the greatest mission opportunity the church has ever known. Above all, this means verbal witness to non-Christians, planting churches where there are none and ministering in Christ's name to a wide range of human needs. Our homes must be "embassies for Christ" and our churches centers where members are called into tangible ministries among the people of all nations.

III

We call for the evangelization of children and youth—within and outside our churches—where substance abuse, broken homes, sexual immorality and suicide ruin vulnerable lives and breed hopelessness. Many are drawn into cults because of the absence of vital Christianity. Our United Methodist Church is ill-prepared to reach this neglected generation and to channel their energies toward the Kingdom of God.

IV

We acknowledge that Christ draws all his followers into lives of personal holiness which undergirds our witness in word and deed. The Holy Spirit empowers believers to manifest the gifts of the Spirit in service and the fruit of the Spirit in their character. The call to moral integrity and self-control is critical for the church's mission. Heterosexual promiscuity and homosexual involvement are both incompatible with the life of holiness and wholeness to which all disciples are called.

V

We deplore our church's defection from its essential Wesleyan Doctrine. The crisis of the United Methodist Church today is a lack of biblical authority and a flawed theology. We must resist imposing upon the church any agenda as a substitute for the central themes of the gospel. The church's preoccupation with the socio-political arena has diminished its credibility and influence in the world. Our faith has come to us at the cost of the lives of saints and martyrs. We must not pass to succeeding generations a gospel which is distorted or defective.

VI

We pray for bold new leadership in the church. We reject the assumption that continued membership decline is inevitable, and we deplore easy rationalizations which evade the crisis. Two decades of decline is unacceptable and calls for church-wide repentance. Today's leadership must be characterized by spiritual maturity and apostolic vision. We call on leaders at every level—bishops, pastors, laity—to train our membership in serious Bible study and in tasks of missions and evangelism. The world is forever our parish!

Therefore, we offer this Declaration to all who love our church. We urge United Methodists everywhere to pray for renewal and faithfulness to the gospel. Because God has been gracious in bringing us to this moment of crisis and action, we commend these concerns to the church. We will work with the Spirit of God in any steps required for change.

Appendix V:
The Memphis Declaration

. . . .

ON *January 24-25, 1992, more than 100 United Methodist clergy and laity gathered in Memphis, Tennessee, to issue a declaration affirming the United Methodist Church's traditional stance on human sexuality and calling the church to a new emphasis on mission and world-wide evangelism.*

The document, named the "Memphis Declaration," was drafted on a Friday and Saturday at the Sheraton Airport Inn in Memphis. It became a rallying point for issues which would be addressed at United Methodism's upcoming General Conference to be held May 5-15 in Louisville, Kentucky.

Rev. Maxie Dunnam, senior minister at Christ United Methodist Church, Memphis, at the time of the gathering, served as host pastor and chairman of the Coordinating Committee. The May/June, 1992, issue of Good News reported some 200,327 affirmative signatures to the Memphis Declaration and total signatures finally exceeded 212,000, representing one of the largest grass-roots expressions ever in United Methodist history. Max and June Goldman of Spirit Lake, Iowa, graciously took responsibility for receiving and counting signatures as they came in.

Speaking at a news conference at the 1992 General Conference in Louisville, Dunnam reported that they received signatures from churches of all sizes from every state in the union and every jurisdiction in United Methodism. The declaration was also endorsed by boards and committees of local churches. "They expressed the hope they see in this for the renewal of the church," said Dunnam.

David Stanley, a lay delegate from Iowa, said about those who had signed the Declaration, "These are people in the pews back home who love our church. They are deeply concerned about the direction of the church and are calling it to faithfulness to the Wesleyan tradition."

The Coordinating Committee for the Memphis Declaration included the following pastors and lay persons: Dr. Jim Buskirk, Mr. Phillip Connolly, Dr. Maxie Dunnam, Dr. Ira Gallaway, Mrs. June Parker Goldman, Mr. Gus Gustafson, Dr. William Hinson, Dr. James Holsinger, Jr., Dr. J. William Jones, Dr. Evelyn Laycock, Dr. John Ed Mathison, Dr. Ed Robb, Jr., Mr. David M. Stanley, and Mr. Paul D. White.

* * * * *

THE MEMPHIS DECLARATION

In his preface to the *Standard Sermons,* John Wesley wrote, "I design plain truth for plain people." Those of us gathered here today in Memphis, lay and clergy alike, seek to emulate Wesley and speak "plain words of truth" to affirm and live out the mandate of Jesus Christ to be his disciples and to call all persons of every race and nation to name and follow him as Savior and Lord.

In the tradition of The Houston Declaration, we come together to challenge United Methodists to live more faithfully as the body of Jesus Christ, under his lordship. This involves confessing, proclaiming and living the Apostolic faith.

In light of the authority of Scripture, we affirm that:

1. God revealed himself in Jesus Christ, the only way of divine salvation.
2. Holy living is the way for Christians to live out the mandate of discipleship given by Jesus Christ.
3. The local congregation is the center for mission and ministry to the world.

GOD'S REVELATION IN JESUS CHRIST

Among the people called Christian—in many nations and among many peoples—including United Methodist, there has been a falling away from commitment to the basic truths and doctrines of the Christian faith.

If we are to be obedient to the teaching of Scripture and to our Wesleyan heritage, we must lift up Jesus Christ as God's gift of salvation offered to all humanity. There are doctrinal issues on which Christians may disagree. We dare not, however, deny our Lord in the name of a shallow pluralism or in a vain attempt to elevate tolerance above primary faith commitment to Jesus Christ. We must not surrender the uniqueness and centrality of Jesus Christ and our Christian heritage for the sake of an easy dialogue with those who are not yet Christian, or a false ecumenism with those who do not profess the fullness of the Christian faith.

Jesus of Nazareth was God in human flesh who lived on earth, suffered and died on the cross, was raised from the dead, lives as eternal Savior and Redeemer, present with us in the person of the Holy Spirit, and He will return again. He is God's only way of salvation. We are called to live out and share this faith personally and collectively as our primary purpose and commitment.

We affirm the call of Jesus Christ, the teaching of holy Scripture, and the faithful witness of John Wesley, that as Christians we are called to holy living. We cannot be self-righteous, because our own personal lives fall far short of his standard of holy living, but the standard must be upheld.

The power of Jesus Christ is at work in the person of the Holy Spirit and can transform every life and overcome every sin. He calls his Church to transform the current culture, not conform to it.

We urge all United Methodists, including ourselves, to turn away from a consumer mentality, greed, and moral disintegration. We are called to be servants and witnesses to our neighbors in word and deed, leading the world to repent and accept Jesus Christ as Savior and Lord.

The Church must reach out in a ministry of love, compassion, and healing to all persons—married, single, children, one-parent homes, and broken families. We affirm marriage as the God-ordained pattern of relationship between men and women. God created us male and female, and the natural order of creation and procreation is the union of male and female as husband and wife. The Christian Church has always held this to be in accordance with God's will. We challenge the Church to be unequivocal in support of the Christian family, the sanctity of human life, and Christian sexual morality: fidelity in marriage and celibacy in singleness.

Scripture plainly identifies adultery, fornication and homosexual practice as sins of the flesh (signs and consequences of the fallen condition of humankind that needs redemption). Let us cease to debate homosexual practice as if the witness of the Scripture and the tradition of the Church were not clear from the beginning. A militant minority must not be allowed to control the direction of the Church of Jesus Christ.

It is time for us to move on to the central purpose of the Church: to serve the world in Jesus Christ's name and win the world for Him.

LOCAL CONGREGATION

The local church is the primary place where we encounter the risen Lord. It must again become, in doctrine and practice, the center of the mission and ministry of the Church. The purpose of the boards, agencies and seminaries must be focused on the equipping of the people of God to be in ministry where they worship and work.

Fiscal responsibility calls for the curtailment, reordering, and reduction of the bureaucracy of the Church so that more of our tithes and offerings will go directly into mission and ministry and *not* increasingly into general church staff and support for boards, agencies and study commissions.

We are concerned about ministerial leadership. We must be especially careful that a seminary education be consistent with our Wesleyan heritage and not dominated by a secular mind-set. Some of our seminaries are committed to both the teaching and modeling of our Wesleyan heritage, recognizing that seminaries are places where men and women are trained for Christian ministry. We celebrate their faithfulness to the Church and we pledge our loyalty and support to them.

CALL TO ACTION

We urge the 1992 General Conference to take these actions and pass necessary legislation to:

1. Reaffirm the use of Biblical language and images in our common life together; mandate the use of the name Father, Son, and Holy Spirit whenever we speak of the Trinity; and reject the replacement of Biblical language and images in the proposed *Book of Worship*, and in other church materials, with alternative language and images which alter the Apostolic faith.

2. Abolish the General Council on Ministries as an unnecessary and costly layer of bureaucracy. It is in direct conflict with the Constitution of the Church, which assigns to the Council of Bishops "the general oversight and promotion of the temporal and spiritual interest of the entire Church and for carrying into effect the rules, regulations, and responsibilities prescribed and enjoined by the General Conference" (Par. 50, Art. III, The Constitution).

3. Reduce the number, size, staff and costs of General Church boards and agencies.

4. Restore the Church's mission and evangelistic thrust. Establish a General Board of Evangelism, including the transfer of the section on church extension from the National Division of the Board of Global Ministries, so that reaching the world for Christ will again be central to the purpose and mission of the Church.

5. Approve the recommendation of the Study Commission and mandate the move of the General Board of Global Ministries out of New York, to enhance the mission and ministry of the Church.

6. Reaffirm Christian sexual morality and the current provisions of the United Methodist Discipline (Par. 71f., 402.2, 906.12). Homosexual persons are people of sacred worth to whom we are called to minister. Since the practice of homosexuality is, however, incompatible with Christian teaching, we call for the rejection of the report and recommendations of the Committee to Study Homosexuality, and oppose further official study. The Biblical witness and the unbroken tradition of the Church provide the foundation of our understanding.

7. Affirm that baptism is a means of God's grace, but that a personal decision to accept Jesus Christ as Savior and Lord is essential for salvation and for full membership in the Church.

Appendix VI: The Invitation to the Church/The Confessing Movement within the United Methodist Church

. . . .

On April 5-6, 1994, a group of 92 United Methodists gathered in Atlanta, Georgia, to consult about the future of The United Methodist Church. Those attending were evangelical, traditionalist and moderate United Methodists all concerned about addressing the liberal trend they fear could split the denomination.

The three prominent United Methodist leaders who brought the group together included: Bishop William R. Cannon (retired) of Atlanta; Rev. Maxie Dunnam, pastor of Christ United Methodist Church in Memphis and president-elect of Asbury Theological Seminary; and Rev. Thomas C. Oden, professor of theology at Drew Theological School.

The 92 participants included bishops, seminary professors, pastors, some members of the World Methodist Council, and prominent laity from all five U.S. jurisdictions of the United Methodist Church. The group issued a statement, called "An Invitation to the Church," which said, in part, that only by recovering a biblically based historic faith that emphasizes the centrality of Christ can the church "avoid schism and prevent mass exodus."

Planners of the event said they expected to go beyond written documents to designing and implementing a grassroots strategy to affect the church directly. "In order to enact the Discipline's call to 'doctrinal reinvigoration,' and to avoid schism and prevent mass exodus, we intend to form a

Confessing Movement within the United Methodist Church,"
the Invitation statement said. "By this we mean people and
congregations who exalt the Lordship of Jesus Christ alone,
and adhere to the doctrinal standards of our church."

Dr. Tom Oden, one of the three convenors, decried what
he termed "already a profound division" in the church, and
said the group wants to develop a broad coalition of "traditionalists and centrists who are unwilling to see the confession of Jesus Christ as Lord and Savior become neglected in
our Christian teaching." Bishop Richard C. Looney of Macon,
Georgia, expressed a concern of many about "how we hold
ourselves accountable for what we've already decided in the
Discipline. We work hard at coming to positions we feel good
about, and then people go their own route."

In addition to Looney and Cannon, four other United
Methodist bishops attended the meeting: Mack B. Stokes, retired, of Atlanta; Earl G. Hunt, retired, of Lake Junaluska,
North Carolina; Felton M. May of Harrisburg, Pennsylvania;
and William Morris of Montgomery, Alabama.

What follows is the full text of "An Invitation to the
Church" released at the Atlanta meeting. The statement was
distributed first to the Council of Bishops, then to the church's
general agencies, and then to the church at large. United Methodists throughout the church were invited to sign it. Dr. John
Ed Mathison was elected as Chairman of the Steering Committee of the Confessing Movement. Other national gather-
ings have been held and The Confessing Movement Within the
United Methodist Church now has an office and full-time staff
in Indianapolis, Indiana.

* * * * *

AN INVITATION TO THE CHURCH

. . . .

WHICH LED TO

THE CONFESSING MOVEMENT WITHIN THE UNITED METHODIST CHURCH

. . . .

I

The United Methodist church is at the crossroads. We face the peril of abandoning the Christian faith, thereby becoming unfaithful disciples of Jesus Christ, or we can embrace the promise of becoming God's instrument in a new awakening of vital Christianity. The causes of the crisis are complex and multiple. However, we believe that the central cause is our abandonment of the truth of the gospel of Jesus Christ as revealed in Scripture and asserted in the classic Christian tradition and historic ecumenical creeds. Specifically we have equivocated regarding the person of Jesus Christ and his atoning work as the unique Savior of the world. We have been distracted by false gospels, and compromised in our mission to declare the true gospel to all people and spread scriptural holiness. For the sake of the kingdom of God, it is now time for action.

II

The renewal, reform and healing of our church can come only through the life-giving power of the Holy Spirit. We cannot yet see clearly how God will lead us along this path. However, with John Wesley, we affirm the apostolic faith of the universal Church together with those Wesleyan distinctives which give form to our faith, as articulated in the doctrinal standards of our own church (viz., the Articles and Confession of Faith, Wesley's *Standard Sermons* and *Explanatory Notes*). These constitute the essential, unchangeable truths of our tradition. We gladly own this anew for ourselves and seek to reclaim it for our whole church.

III

Under God's judgment and by God's grace we covenant to participate in the Spirit's reconstruction of the church built upon the foundation of the faith once for all delivered to the saints. We covenant to engage in a revitalized mission which expresses our historic concern for social holiness and fidelity to the fulfillment of the Great Commission. To all United Methodists regardless of race or gender who desire to contend for this faith, we extend an invitation to join us in this endeavor.

In order to enact the *Discipline's* call to "doctrinal reinvigoration," and to avoid schism and prevent mass exodus, we intend to form a Confessing Movement within the United Methodist Church. By this we mean people and congregations who exalt the Lordship of Jesus Christ alone, and adhere to the doctrinal standards of our church.

We call upon all pastors and congregations to join with us in this Confessing Movement, and to challenge and equip their people as agents of God's kingdom.

We look to the Council of Bishops for doctrinal oversight according to paragraph 514.2 "to guard, transmit, teach and proclaim corporately and individually the apostolic faith as it is expressed in Scripture and Tradition, and as they are led and endowed by the Spirit to interpret that faith evangelically and prophetically." In particular we ask the bishops to affirm their own teaching authority and to declare our church's commitment to Jesus Christ as the only Lord and Savior of the World.

We call upon seminaries of our church to transmit the historic Christian faith. We call upon the boards and agencies of the church to fulfill their primary role of being servants of the local church.

IV

The crisis we discern extends beyond our denomination. We witness similar strains and struggles among our sisters and brothers in all the churches of the West. Because we are baptized into the one universal Church, and because the problems we face will best be resolved by utilizing the gifts God gives to the whole community of faith, we rejoice in the stirrings for renewal that we see among other communions. We commit ourselves to praying with them for the coming of the kingdom in our midst.

Bibliography

THEOLOGICAL INTEGRITY AND DOCTRINAL RECOVERY

"Is the United Methodist Church a Confessional Church?", Leicester Longden and John Swomley, in *Perkin's Perspective,* the journal of the Perkins School of Theology.

Pocket Guide to Christian Beliefs, I. Howard Marshall, InterVarsity, 3d ed., 1978.

"German Church Struggle," James R. Edwards, in *Theology Matters,* a Publication of Presbyterians for Faith, Family and Ministry, January/February, 1997.

"A Hope for Collapsing Churches," David Mills, *The Evangelical Catholic,* January/April, 1996.

God in the Dock: Essays on Theology and Ethics, C. S. Lewis, ed. Walter Hooper, Grand Rapids: William B. Eerdmans, 1970.

"What to Do About Other Gospels," Richard John Neuhaus, *Faith and Renewal,* July/August, 1990.

Rekindling the Flame, William H. Willimon and Robert L. Wilson, Abingdon, Nashville, 1987.

Signs and Wonders: The Mighty Work of God in the Church, Richard B. Wilke, Abingdon, Nashville, 1989.

LIBERALISM AND UNITED METHODIST THOUGHT

Meeting Jesus Again for the First Time, Marcus J. Borg.

The Empty Church: The Suicide of Liberal Christianity, Thomas C. Reeves, The Free Press, 1996.

Unity, Liberty, and Charity: Building Bridges Under Icy Waters, ed. William J. Abraham and Donald E. Messer, Abingdon, Nashville.

Theological Transition in American Methodism: 1790–1935, Robert E. Chiles, Abingdon, Nashville, 1965.

Defending the Faith; J. Gresham Machen and the Crisis of Conservative Protestantism in Modern America, D. G. Hart, The Johns Hopkins University Press, 1994.

"Have We Lost Our Way?", Sam Moffett, in *ReNews,* a Publication of Presbyterians for Renewal.

"The Fatal Apostasy of the Modern Church," Edwin Lewis, *Religion in Life II* (Autumn 1933), pp. 483–92.

The Kingdom of God in America, H. Richard Niebuhr, The Shoe String Press, Hamden, Conn., 1956.

Methodism and Society in the Twentieth Century, Walter G. Muelder, Vol. II of the *Methodism and Society* series, Abingdon, Nashville, 1961.

"At the Crossroads of Dogma," R. R. Reno, in *Pro Ecclesia: A Journal of Catholic and Evangelical Theology,* Vol. II, No. 1, Winter, 1993.

"An Analysis of Major Issues Addressed by the 1988 General Conference," a study published by the General Council on Ministries of the United Methodist Church, Dayton, Ohio, fall, 1988.

The Erosion of Truth and Disappointments of Dialogue

Reclaiming the Great Tradition: Evangelicals, Catholics & Orthodox in Dialogue, ed. James S. Cutsinger, InterVarsity, Downers Grove, Ill., 1997.

Requiem: A Lament in Three Movements, Thomas C. Oden, Abingdon, Nashville, 1995.

"Crisis in the Church," Thomas F. Torrance, *Theological Digest & Outlook*, No. 2, July 1991, pp. 1–6.

"Three Cheers for Our Evangelical Brothers and Sisters," Tom Griffith, *Open Hands*, Winter, 1995, journal of the Reconciling Congregations Program.

An Evangelical Faith for Today, John Lawson, Abingdon, Nashville, 1972.

A Passion for Truth: The Intellectual Coherence of Evangelicalism, Alister McGrath, InterVarsity, Downers Grove, Ill., 1996.

The Closing of the American Mind, Allan Bloom, Simon and Schuster, New York, 1987.

Ethics, Dietrich Bonhoeffer.

THE HOMOSEXUALITY CONTROVERSY
AND ITS DEEPER MEANING

"Blessing the Unblessable," David A. Seamands, *Good News*, May/June 1998.

Romans: God's Good News for the World, John R. W. Stott, InterVarsity, 1994.

"Love, No Matter What," Richard John Neuhaus, *First Things*, No. 76, October, 1997, pp. 81–85.

"Homosexuality and the Scripture," Wolfhart Pannenberg, *Good News*, March/April, 1997, pp. 26–27. (Originally printed in *Church Times* in Britain.)

Churches in Covenant Communion: The Church of Christ Uniting, approved and recommended to the churches by the Seventeenth Plenary of the Consultation on Church Union, New Orleans, December 9, 1988.

Rescuing the Bible from Fundamentalism: A Bishop Rethinks the Meaning of Scripture, John Shelby Spong, Harper & Row, San Francisco, 1991.

Daily Christian Advocate, May 4, 1988, p. 456.

Women-Church: Theology and Practice of Feminist Liturgical Communities, Rosemary Radford Ruether, Harper & Row, 1985.

RADICAL FEMINISM—THE UNCHALLENGED CONTROVERSY

"A Christian Women's Declaration," published by the Ecumenical Coalition on Women and Society, 1521 Sixteenth St., NW, Suite 300, Washington, D.C. 20036

Christian Feminism: Visions of a New Humanity, ed. Judith Weidman, Harper & Row, 1984.

"An Open Letter to Presbyterians," a letter from six professors of Princeton Theological Seminary.

Wisdom's Feast: Sophia in Study and Celebration, Susan Cady, Marian Ronan and Hal Taussig, Harper & Row, San Francisco, 1986.